CW01334329

Neuroparenting

Jan Macvarish

Neuroparenting

The Expert Invasion of Family Life

palgrave
macmillan

Jan Macvarish
University of Kent
United Kingdom

ISBN 978-1-137-54732-3   ISBN 978-1-137-54733-0 (eBook)
DOI 10.1057/978-1-137-54733-0

Library of Congress Control Number: 2016945181

© The Editor(s) (if applicable) and The Author(s) 2016
The author(s) has/have asserted their right(s) to be identified as the author(s) of this work in accordance with the Copyright, Designs and Patents Act 1988.
This work is subject to copyright. All rights are solely and exclusively licensed by the Publisher, whether the whole or part of the material is concerned, specifically the rights of translation, reprinting, reuse of illustrations, recitation, broadcasting, reproduction on microfilms or in any other physical way, and transmission or information storage and retrieval, electronic adaptation, computer software, or by similar or dissimilar methodology now known or hereafter developed.
The use of general descriptive names, registered names, trademarks, service marks, etc. in this publication does not imply, even in the absence of a specific statement, that such names are exempt from the relevant protective laws and regulations and therefore free for general use.
The publisher, the authors and the editors are safe to assume that the advice and information in this book are believed to be true and accurate at the date of publication. Neither the publisher nor the authors or the editors give a warranty, express or implied, with respect to the material contained herein or for any errors or omissions that may have been made.

Cover illustration: Détail de la Tour Eiffel © nemesis2207/Fotolia.co.uk

Printed on acid-free paper

This Palgrave Macmillan imprint is published by Springer Nature
The registered company is Macmillan Publishers Ltd. London

Acknowledgements

Much of the research which informs this book was conducted with Dr Ellie Lee, Reader of Social Policy at the School of Social Policy, Sociology and Social Research at the University of Kent, and Dr Pam Lowe, Senior Lecturer in Sociology at Aston University, for the project 'Biologising Parenting: Neuroscience Discourse and English Social and Public Health Policy'. I therefore thank Ellie and Pam and our funder, the Faraday Institute's 'Uses and Abuses of Biology' programme (2011–14).

I also thank my other associates at the Centre for Parenting Culture Studies at the University of Kent, Jennie Bristow, Charlotte Faircloth and Frank Furedi, for the intellectual inspiration, stimulation and friendship they have provided over the years and for their invaluable feedback on an earlier draft of this book. To return to Ellie, I thank her especially for the unstinting support she has provided during our many collaborations at Kent. Her passion for scholarship combines with an absolute commitment to an outward-looking sense of purpose to create a uniquely collegial and inspiring culture in our virtual 'centre'.

Finally, I thank my family. My parents Ann and Alasdair Macvarish are the ultimate role models not just in this parenting lark, but in living a good life in the fullest sense. My husband Mark Birbeck with whom I embarked on the project of making a family almost 20 years ago, I still consider to be head and shoulders above any other human being I know. Our sons Louis and Reuben have given us the thrill of feeling responsible for creating new human life while continually surprising us with the incredible power of human individuality.

Contents

1 What Is Neuroparenting? 1

2 The Claims of Neuroparenting 19

3 Neuroparenting and the Quest for Natural Authority 41

4 Neuroparenting and the State 61

5 Getting Inside the Family 77

6 The Problem with Neuroparenting 95

Index 113

List of Figures

Fig. 1.1 Front covers of the UK government reports, Early
Intervention: The Next Steps (Allen, January 2011a)
and Early Intervention: Smart investment, massive savings
(Allen, July 2011b) Crown Copyright 2011   3

CHAPTER 1

What Is Neuroparenting?

Abstract Neuroparenting is a way of thinking which claims that 'we now know' (by implication, once and for all) how children ought to be raised. The basis for this final achievement of certainty regarding child-rearing is said to be discoveries made through neuroscience about the development of the human brain, in particular, during infancy. Macvarish situates the rise of neuroparenting in the UK policy domain within a broader context in which the idea of a parenting deficit has taken hold of policy-makers' imaginations and parent training has become increasingly normalised through new institutional structures and government programmes, notably those of early intervention. The particular power of neuroparenting lies in its appeal to the authority of the fashionable claims of neuroscience and its promise to make material, and even visible, the quality and quantity of parental love.

Keywords Neuroparenting • Child-rearing • Parenting • Parenting culture • Family policy • Early years policy • Parenting support • Early intervention • Neuroscience • Brains • Love

This is a book about how we raise our children, or more precisely, it is a book about what we think we are doing when we raise our children. The way we understand this most vital of human tasks is shaped by our fundamental understandings of what kind of creatures human beings are, how we live with one another in society and how, via the movement from one generation to the next, human history is moved along from the present to the

© The Editor(s) (if applicable) and The Author(s) 2016 1
J. Macvarish, *Neuroparenting*,
DOI 10.1057/978-1-137-54733-0_1

future. Shifts in any of these interrelated conceptualisations have ideological and practical repercussions for what we do to bring the next generation to adulthood. Therefore, by looking closely at the discourse through which changes to the culture and practices of child-rearing are argued for in the domain of politics and public policy, we can deepen our understanding of the particular historical conjuncture in which we currently stand.

There is a long history of advice given to parents to guide them in the task of socialising the next generation (Furedi 2001, 2008; Hardyment 1995; Hendrick 1997; Stearn 2003) but we will look at a new addition, 'neuroparenting'. Neuroparenting is a way of thinking which claims that 'we now know' (by implication, once and for all) how children ought to be raised. The basis for this final achievement of certainty regarding childrearing, which we know has changed dramatically from one historical period to the next and which we are aware still varies greatly across diverse human societies, is said to be discoveries made through neuroscience about the development of the human brain, in particular, during infancy. One neuroparenting proponent, Dr Erin Clabough (2016), aims to raise 'parental awareness about normal brain development' because 'every day is a critical period' (see www.neuroparent.org).

Readers may not have heard of neuroparenting. This is not surprising, as it is a neologism which so far exists primarily in the branding of a handful of such 'parenting experts', whose advice, they claim, is informed by the latest brain research. However, new parents are very likely to have heard 'brain claims' about the 'critical' significance of what they do in pregnancy and the 'early years' of their child's life for his or her long-term prospects. All of us, parents or not, will have heard about studies showing that breast milk or classical music have brain-boosting properties or that child abuse and neglect have brain-shrinking effects. Anyone working in the public sector, in particular in education, the early years, maternal and child health or social services, will have been told of the proven benefits of 'early intervention', which works because it takes advantage of the 'window of opportunity' represented by the years 0–5, 0–3, 0–2 or minus 9 months to 1.

What 'we now know' about the infant brain is described using neurovocabulary such as neurons, synapses, critical periods, toxic stress and cortisol. The case for urgent action will possibly have been emphasised using an image of two brains, one 'normal' the other smaller and containing 'black holes', with the explanation given that the normal-sized brain is the product of parental love and the shrivelled one is the product of parental neglect (seen here on the cover of two UK government reports, this image is referred to henceforth as the 'Perry image' owing to its source, neuroparenting advocate Professor Bruce D. Perry) (Fig. 1.1).

Early Intervention: The Next Steps

An Independent Report to Her Majesty's Government
Graham Allen MP

3 Year Old Children

Normal   Extreme Neglect

January 2011   HM Government

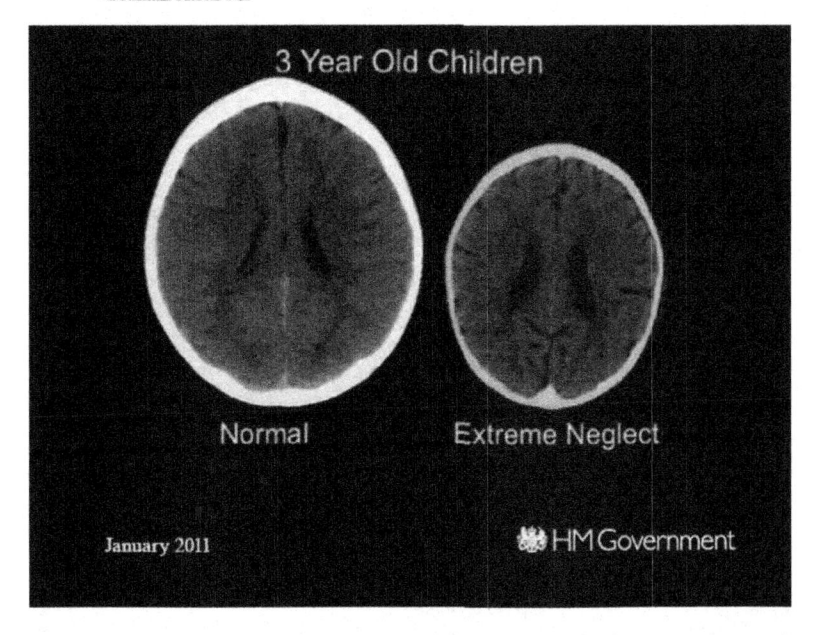

Fig. 1.1 Front covers of the UK government reports, Early Intervention: The Next Steps (Allen, January 2011a) and Early Intervention: Smart investment, massive savings (Allen, July 2011b) Crown Copyright 2011

Babies' brains are just one element in contemporary parenting discourse, but the underlying message of neuroparenting, that the early years 'last forever' and therefore deserve much greater parental and societal attention, is ubiquitous. Concern for babies' brains has entered the mainstream of British politics over the past decade. As this book was being edited, the British Prime Minister (PM) David Cameron gave a speech entitled 'Life Chances', the rhetorical cornerstone of which was brain claiming: 'Thanks

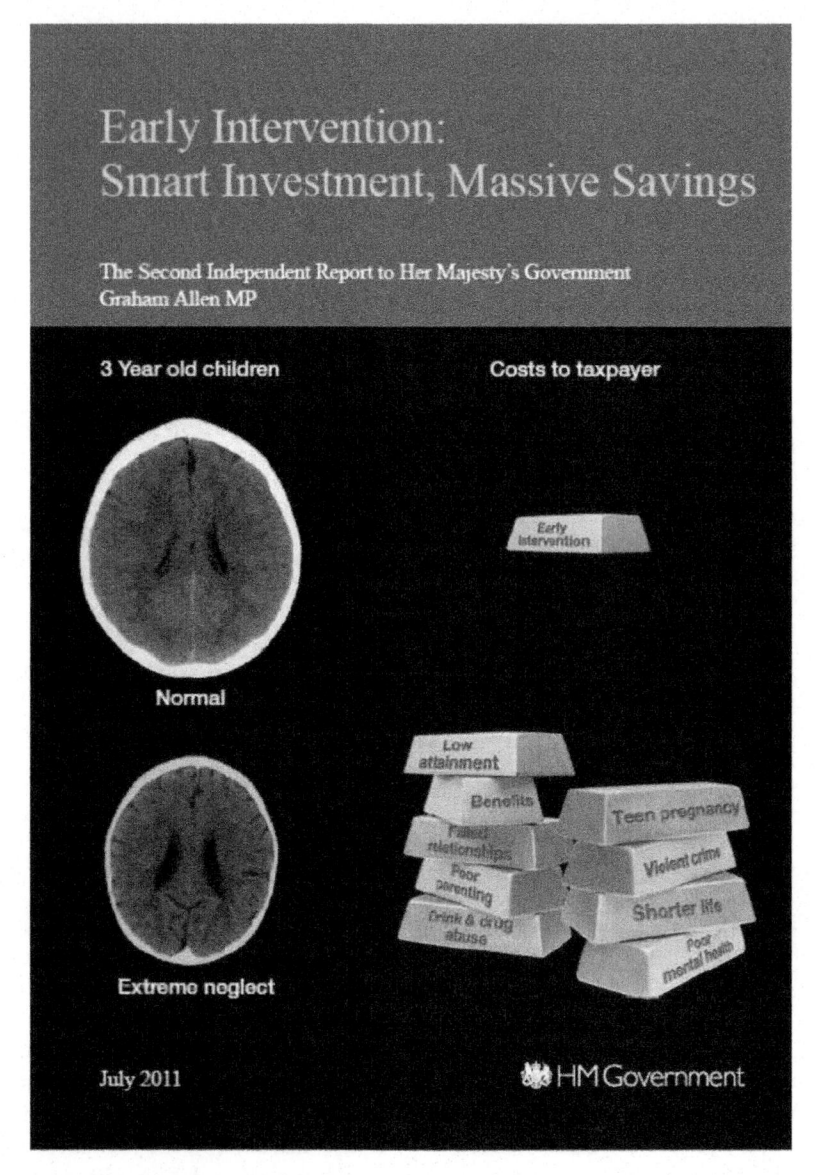

Fig. 1.1 Continued

to the advent of functional MRI scanners, neuroscientists and biologists say they have learnt more about how the brain works in the last 10 years than in the rest of human history put together.' He went on to argue, 'when neuroscience shows us the pivotal importance of the first few years of life in determining the adults we become, we must think much more radically about improving family life and the early years'. Drawing on the lexicon of neuro-buzzwords, he justified the provision of parenting classes for all UK parents on the basis that 'one critical finding is that the vast majority of the synapses, the billions of connections that carry information through our brains, develop in the first 2 years. Destinies can be altered for good or ill in this window of opportunity' (Cameron 2016).

The 'Life Chances' speech is the clearest expression yet in mainstream British politics of a 'brainified' argument for government action. Many on social media reacted angrily, objecting that David Cameron was in no position to be dishing out parenting advice, that he was just a privileged 'toff' who spent much of his own childhood away from his parents at boarding school. Numerous commentators mockingly reminded us that the PM and his wife had once driven off after a pub lunch without their eight year-old daughter. A few took the speech's references to the importance of marriage and the problem of absent dads as evidence of the 'same old' Tory-moralising, while others concluded that Cameron was blaming parents for failing to cope with the cuts to welfare and services that his government was implementing. But what nobody (with the exception of Lee 2016) reflected on was just how remarkable (and absurd) it was to hear the British PM propose that the best solution to the very grown-up problems of economic and social malaise was the project of getting British mothers and fathers to engage in more of 'the baby talk, the silly faces, the chatter even when we know they can't answer back' through which 'mums and dads literally build babies' brains', as though what he called 'the biological power of love, trust and security' would then automatically emanate from individual babies to the structures of British society (Cameron 2016).

This book therefore conceptualises neuroparenting as a political argument. The rhetoric of babies' brains is deployed to challenge the fundamental rights and responsibilities which have shaped British family life for the past 100 years or more, in particular, the general presumption that parents know best when it comes to caring for babies and getting toddlers to school age. The pre-school years have traditionally been a time when parents, and mothers in particular, were entrusted with almost exclusive care of the child and were left to perform this task amongst themselves, making use of wider relationships with family, friends and community. Recourse to medical advice and socialised child care was on the parent's terms and heavy state intervention to rescue the child occurred only when things went very badly wrong. But the neuroparenting argument reconstructs this period of informal, privatised care as being of national importance and therefore as everybody's business. Now considered to be precariously full of risks and yet more important than any other period in the life course, the early years are, as David Cameron claimed, said to determine our 'destinies' for 'good or ill'. The neuroparenting argument that 'the first years last for ever' has grown in strength in recent years as it has been repeated in many public forums: in parliamentary inquiries and debates, on government committees and in published reports, in think-tank documents and during symposiums, at guest lectures by international neuroparenting 'celebrities' and in the pages of national newspapers. In the rest of the book, we refer to the promotion of neuroparenting within the policy domain in a number of ways. We make use of the concept 'the first three years movement' (Thornton 2011a, b) to describe its growing influence and will also use, interchangeably, the terms '0–3', the 'early years' or the 'parenting support' agenda.

Normalising Parent Training

While David Cameron's speech provides the most explicit evidence yet that the neuroparenting agenda has been adopted by UK policy-makers, it should be understood as the result of a much longer process of political change. The fact that when a Conservative PM confidently called for all parents to offer themselves up for state-provided training there were only a few limp cries of 'it's the nanny state gone mad' in response, indicates the extent to which the argument for ending the presumption of parental competence and the right to a private family life has already been won amongst the political class at least. The argument that the boundaries around the family need to be weakened in the name of children's welfare has been going on since at least the mid-1990s. As time has gone on, its proponents have become less apologetic and oppositional voices have become almost non-existent. The Liberal-Democrat peer, Baroness Tyler, in the foreword to a parliamentary report on parenting and social mobility, indicates that politicians are very aware that the parenting support agenda requires a reworking of the presupposition that parents know better than the state when it comes to how they raise their children, when she says, 'For too long, fear of being criticised for interfering in family life has led politicians and policy makers to shy away from this arena.'

Pre-empting David Cameron by almost a year, she states, 'The early years and particularly what happens in the home are of utmost importance for a child's future,' because, 'it is parents—not teachers or government—who are ultimately responsible for a child's development in these early years.' However, we can see that although parents are held totally responsible for raising the next generation, their capacity to perform this vital task is called into question:

> The hope has been that all parents would be able to provide the most appropriate social and emotional development for their children in the pre-school years, which we now know is the vital underpinning for educational attainment and emotional wellbeing, without needing any help and support in doing this critically important job…Yet it is time to change our views about parenting: not all parents know how to be a good parent, not because of lack of skills or bad intentions, but often because of poor information, advice and support… In short it is time to end the 'last great taboo in public policy'. (Tyler 2015)

While many people might share Baroness Tyler's concerns regarding the ability of *some* parents to raise their children well, it is unlikely that they would be happy for this doubt from on high to be applied to themselves. But the parenting support agenda is a universal one, as David Cameron made clear:

> getting parenting and the early years right isn't just about the hardest-to-reach families, frankly it's about everyone. We all have to work at it…As we know, they don't come with a manual and that's obvious, but is it right that all of us get so little guidance?…We all need more help with this – because it is the most important job we'll ever have. So I believe we now need to think about how to make it normal – even aspirational to attend parenting classes. (Cameron 2016)

Some parents might agree that raising their children is 'the most important job they'll ever have', but they may disagree that 'teachers and government' are totally insignificant when it comes to what will shape their child's future. It is yet to be seen whether substantial numbers will be convinced to pursue their parental aspirations through parent training; certainly, the signs so far are that very few people think this way. The CANparent trial, launched in 2011 in some regions of the UK, sought to 'de-stigmatise' attendance at parenting classes by offering free vouchers via Boots the Chemist. Despite the claim, made at its launch, that three-quarters of parents want information and support, after two years, the programme had embarrassingly low levels of take-up; only 4 % of eligible parents redeemed their vouchers (Richardson 2014; Lee et al. 2014b). However, even if parents do not themselves wish to attend parent training, the proposition that it is necessary (albeit for other, worse, parents) may be widely shared. What the attempts at normalising parent training in the initial CANparent trial and the recent announcement of a national roll-out, despite lack of popular demand, show is that the relatively widespread belief that British parents 'could do better' can now be operationalised by a body of individuals and organisations with a financial stake in providing state-funded parent training, no matter what. They will continue to rework the marketing and mode of delivery of their services to build demand.

The relationship between neuroparenting and the attempt to normalise parent training is made very clear in the '1001 Critical Days' campaign, launched in 2013 by a group of Members of Parliament (MPs) from all political parties. In an introduction to the campaign's first manifesto, the Chief Medical Officer for England and Wales, Sally Davies, states:

> Science is helping us to understand how love and nurture by caring adults is hard wired into the brains of children. We know too that not intervening now will affect not just this generation of children and young people but also the next. Those who suffer multiple adverse childhood events achieve less educationally, earn less, and are less healthy, making it more likely that the cycle of harm is perpetuated, in the following generation. (Davies 2013)

This exemplifies another pivotal 'brain claim'; that poor parental nurture results in not only familial unhappiness, but more politically graspable social problems such as a lack of educational attainment, low wages and ill health. The spectre of the continual reproduction of dysfunctional individuals, families and communities at the bottom of society is raised to make the case for ever-earlier intervention as an urgent social necessity. Arguing that 'cycles of harm' can only be broken by early intervention in parenting, policy-makers make the case not just for universal, voluntary parent training but for its compulsory imposition on the most 'troubled families'. According to this view, intervention can never happen too early. In the foreword to the '1001 Critical Days' 'Building Great Britons' report (2015), MP Tim Loughton suggested that what we really need is a 'pre-troubled families programme', because:

> This is not 'rocket science'. Technically it is 'neuro-science'. As a concept it is at last gaining wider acceptance with policy makers and clinicians brave enough to take a longer term view of how intervening early, even before a child is born, is the best way of that child growing up to be a well-rounded member of society. (Loughton 2015, p. 3)

The Requirements of Neuroparenting

Neuroparenting manifests itself in various ways, but the shared theme is that new knowledge about the brain provides us with novel, refreshed or more urgent rationales not just for social action but for change at the level of individual behaviour in the most intimate ways that parents relate to their children. When it comes to the everyday business of caring for infants, the requirements of neuroparenting can be summarised as follows:

1. The parent should actively endeavour emotionally to 'attune' themselves to their baby through eye contact, touch and verbal interaction.
2. This attunement can, and must, begin in utero through communicating with the foetus and doing everything possible to protect it from harm.
3. The parent should follow the infant's lead in the attunement process, as the baby is 'hard-wired' to expect care and attention from its caregivers.
4. The parent should continually respond to the visual and auditory cues which express the infant's needs, not just for food, sleep or nappy-changing, but for emotional comfort and security.
5. Neuroparenting demands that the parent sees themselves as their child's 'first teacher', with the developmental process requiring active, conscious and educated nurturing. This means talking, singing and reading to the child from conception onwards, with the infant brain in mind.
6. Development is a process of hardwiring the physical structures of the brain, but these physical structures are formed through a social relationship of love and care. If the parent does not adopt this mode of parent–infant care, there is a risk that the child will not achieve normal neurological development.

What the reader will notice from the instructions above is that they somewhat nebulously describe what modern parents already do: meeting their baby's wants and needs, looking into their eyes, talking to them, touching them, singing to them and reading them stories. The neuro-informed wisdom turns out to translate into pretty banal repetitions of all contemporary parenting advice in its most generalised form. This is what is so fascinating about neuroparenting. For all the apparent novelty of brain science and the new vocabulary of synapses and neurons, it actually requires parents only to *do more* and to *do earlier* what they already do.

In its emphasis on attunement and attachment, neuroparenting has much in common with what popular parenting authors William and Martha Sears termed 'Attachment Parenting' back in the 1980s. The Sears describe certain practices of infant care as necessary for attachment parenting: primarily breastfeeding, holding babies a lot and practising 'positive discipline' (by which they meant praising the child for good behaviour rather than punishing bad). Most importantly though, as the Sears explain, attachment parenting is not 'a strict set of rules' but 'an approach to raising children'. Attachment parenting 'means opening your mind and heart to the individual needs of your baby and letting your knowledge of your child be your guide to making on-the-spot decisions about what works best for both of you. In a nutshell, AP is learning to read the cues of your baby and responding appropriately to those cues' (Sears and Sears 2001, p. 2). Readers will notice that what was considered a particular 'parenting style' back in the 1980s, has become the mainstream definition of 'good parenting' today and it has been given a new brain basis in the neuroparenting claim that new knowledge about the brain confirms that this is the correct way to care for babies.

This baby-centred, baby-led child care, which requires parental 'attunement', has been given the label 'intensive parenting' by US sociologist Sharon Hays. She characterises this new approach as 'expert-guided, emotionally absorbing, labor intensive and financially expensive' (Hays 1996, p. 8). Parents must be continually reflective on their own behaviour and dispositions and above all, be aware of the risks of getting it wrong. I, with colleagues at the Centre for Parenting Culture Studies at the University of Kent, have explored this new way of thinking about the task of raising children, a shift in what we term 'contemporary parenting culture' (Lee et al. 2014b).

Our work (Macvarish 2014; Lee et al. 2014a), and that of others, has identified the translation of the intensive parenting imperative into the policy domain since the late 1990s as crucial to 'a radical and qualitative shift' towards 'direct state intervention in parenting' and this has great significance because it has changed the language and the 'framework of ideas' through which the parent–child relationship is understood (Smith 2010, pp. 358–9).

The Power of the Brain

While drawing on the authority of science, neuroparenting is most often advocated not by scientists but by philanthropists, politicians, social activists and 'moral entrepreneurs'. Some of them seem quite unlikely, such as Prince Charles, whose attitude towards science has been ambivalent in the past (Prince of Wales 2000). In a 2009 newspaper interview, the future king took credit for alerting controversial social entrepreneur Camila Batmanghelidjh (founder of the now discredited and disbanded children's charity Kids Company) to the relevance of insights 'from neuroscience' for her work with inner-city children. His Royal Highness claimed to have sent Batmanghelidjh 'a sheaf of 25 clinical papers that looked at the impact of abuse on children's brain development'. The article went on to explain that Batmanghelidjh had since instigated research projects 'which involve scanning the brains of troubled teenagers attending Kids Company', which she believed 'will prove that the brain is altered by early trauma and abuse' (Evening Standard 2009). That neuroparenting is advocated less by parents than by the 'great and the good' has been true from the start.

Brain-based early years activism began in the USA in the early 1990s, and has become increasingly vocal and influential since, achieving legitimacy in the USA, Canada, New Zealand, Australia and the UK, but also becoming embedded within transnational institutions such as the World Health Organisation (WHO), the Organisation for Economic Co-operation and Development (OECD), the European Union and UNICEF. This 'first three years movement' (Thornton 2011a, b) has been described as:

> an alliance of child welfare advocates and politicians which draws on the authority of neuroscience to argue that social problems such as inequality, poverty, educational underachievement, violence and mental illness are best addressed through 'early intervention' programmes to protect or enhance emotional and cognitive aspects of children's brain development. (Macvarish et al. 2014)

The movement tends to make the case for ever-earlier interventions with the promise of saving money 'down the line' on adult services for the mentally ill, the criminal, the addicted, the unemployed and the under-educated. Such services will, it is promised, be rendered unnecessary once human suffering is eradicated at source by the neurological neutralisation of parental harm.

In the case of Camila Batmanghelidjh's Kids Company, the invocation of neuroscience played an important role in creating a unique selling point for her social enterprise's pursuit of private and public funding. Batmanghelidjh's strength lay in her ability to summon up apocalyptic visions of social disintegration and dysfunctional youth, while proposing 'soft' therapeutic solutions reinforced by 'hard' neurotalk of brain scans, stress hormones and frontal lobes. The use of brain vocabulary and brain images seemed to subdue the critical faculties of observers while enabling supporters to feel that they were privy to a novel form of charity action, backed up by both emotive and 'evidence-based' argument. One journalist claimed to have been 'shocked' by Batmanghelidjh's statement that child neglect is worse than child abuse, but went on to describe how she was miraculously converted once shown the Perry image of the two brains:

I quickly understand that she is absolutely correct. Batmanghelidjh shows me a couple of photographs of brain scans, one of a cared-for child and one of a neglected child. She traces her finger round the periphery of the brain of the neglected child, where a white line representing absent neural development can clearly be seen. 'Neglect – continuous lack of love', she says, 'deprives the child of a personal soothing repertoire'. (Orr 2009)

This is the extreme end of neuroparenting; the claim that parent-induced childhood trauma results in damaged brains is deployed as part of a call to action for charitable and state agencies to fund innovative approaches to tackling poverty and social breakdown. But brain claiming is (literally) visible across a spectrum of public domains. The argument that the 'first years last for ever' has been translated into a new arena for universal state action. In the UK, new institutions such as the Early Intervention Foundation have been established, and millions of pounds of funding paid to third-sector enterprises, to train a growing workforce of people in the provision of 'parenting support' (Daly 2013; Gillies 2011; Lewis 2011). These are the midwives, health visitors, social workers, foster carers and early years workers who are routinely shown the Perry pictures of 'healthy' and 'damaged' children's brains, and told that their work supporting parents will not only help to secure the future emotional wellbeing of the nation, but will revolutionise class differentials by increasing social mobility.

The Parenting Deficit

As many have pointed out, the use of the word 'parent' as a verb and the idea of 'parenting' as a noun are relatively recent arrivals in the landscape of child-rearing (Couchman 1983; Faircloth 2013; Furedi 2001; 2008). One scholar suggests that 'parenting' connotes the task of child-rearing in inherently problematic terms as 'something we seem to undertake reluctantly rather than naturally' or as 'a kind of supplement when the natural business of being a father or a mother has broken down' (Smith 2010, p. 360). The parent–child relationship is also 'largely seen as a technical matter' and not 'an easy or comfortable one'. Depicted as 'almost the toughest job human beings have', in the form of parenting, raising children has become a 'rather dour business' and, most importantly for our understanding of neuroparenting, 'one in which experts…have a proper role' (Smith 2010, p. 360).

The deployment of 'neuro' as a prefix to 'parenting' indicates an attempt to root this new, problematised way of talking about family life within an objective, scientific truth. Although historians and social scientists have identified a long history to the scientisation and medicalisation of motherhood from the late nineteenth century onwards (Apple 1995, 2006; Ehrenreich and English 1979; Hulbert 2004), there has been a parallel respect for 'maternal instinct', for the authority of parents and a recognition that families require privacy and autonomy to function as families. Throughout most of the nineteenth and twentieth centuries, the British state was reluctant explicitly to target relationships *within* families, except in outlying cases that were identified as already being 'dysfunctional'. Although of course there were strong social and moral norms towards what outer form the family should take (married, two parents), in most cases, this outer form was taken to be a guarantor of parental responsibility *within* the family. Today, when parental marriage is much less likely to constitute the outer form or the starting point of family living, there is far greater concern for what goes on within (Gillies 2011; Macvarish et al. 2015).

This concern is, to some extent, understandable. Changes to the external structure of family relations have been rapid, but are experienced and interpreted differently by different groups and individuals; what some have called the breakdown of the family, others have celebrated as a diversification which allows increased choice and opportunities for authentic self-expression. The responsibility that one generation must take for the development of another is unsurprisingly a source of worry when the conditions in which it is performed seem to be uncharted waters. However, the way we experience this responsibility, even if we don't see it as any more negotiable than parents ever have, is peculiarly wracked with anxiety today. Back in 1983, the US sociologists Peter and Brigitte Berger felt able to write:

> When a child is born into this world, he seems to enter into it in a natural, effortless fashion. This process of growth is a source of never-ending excitement in the child and of joy to his or her parents. (Berger and Berger 1983, p. 149)

These words from only 30 years ago jar with our twenty-first-century sensibility which has become so accustomed to seeing pregnancy, birth, infancy and childhood as rife with risks, threats and problems. No doubt parents do still experience joy in the anticipation, arrival and development of their children, but they also experience an unprecedented amount of anxiety (Furedi 2001, 2008) and the tasks associated with it seem more numerous, more onerous and more significant than ever before. The proponents of neuroparenting certainly see a child's entry into the world as very far from 'natural' and they display little faith in parental excitement or joy about the new arrival. A major emphasis of the first three years in the UK at the moment is maternal depression, both ante- and postnatal (it is claimed by some that over 70–80 % of new mothers will have mental health problems) and this concern is increasingly being extended to fathers.

Love Biologised

One of the reasons why parenting is now conceived of as such a risky business is that it is thought to be utterly determinate of who or what the child becomes in adulthood. Information produced for maternal and child health professionals by the Department of Health sets out this 'parental determinism' when it states, 'A child's experience and environment—both in the womb and in early life—lay the foundation for life' (DH 2011). The conceptualisation of the foetus and the baby as a straightforward continuum is crucial to the new thinking. It means that parental responsibility is 'extended backwards to conception, and possibly even before' (Lee et al. 2010), in order to create what is sometimes referred to as a 'healthy uterine environment'. It also means that parental culpability is lifelong, as what happens to a child in the earliest years is said to last forever. The same document goes on:

> Mothers and fathers are the most important influence on a child's well-being and development. Loving, caring and secure parenting, as well as good nutrition and protection from toxic substances such as tobacco, are essential for a child's growth, well-being and development. (DH 2011)

The foundational claim of neuroparenting is that the truth of parental determinism has now been revealed through neuroscience. Critical commentators or 'neuroskeptics' often focus their attention on disputing claims that particular parental actions (in particular, the purchase of special 'brain-boosting' toys or digital media) can increase the IQ of babies, seeing this as a reflection of 'neoliberal' values of individual self-advancement. But while a concern for intelligence is a feature of neuroparenting, it actually emerges from an argument precisely against the kind of goal-driven 'pushy' parenting which aims to raise smarter babies. IQ and intelligence are rarely explicitly mentioned in neuroparenting discourse, it is the emotional life of babies and parents that is its target. This is why much of neuroparenting relies on rather old claims concerning the infant's need for 'secure attachment'—a psychological concept which predates neuroscience by almost 50 years, but which, it is now claimed, has been validated by recent brain research. If neuroparenting were solely concerned with intelligence, it would be too one-sided to appeal to most parents, who appreciate and care for their child 'in the round' as a whole being. At the level of politics and public discourse, it would also lack the emotional and moral power needed to make the case for social interventions to prevent the emotional trauma of children whose brains are at risk from this inadequate parenting.

The idea of the brain is not crucial to intensive parenting or parental determinism as both of these predate the interest in neuroscience.

However, neuroscience plays an important role in concretising these new 'oughts' of good parenting—the norms of highly attentive maternal care and the presumption that the early years last forever—by rooting them in the 'is' of biological fact. As such, neuroparenting is not talked of just as another theory or lifestyle to be put into the mix of culturally specific parenting styles, but as a scientifically proven truth which brings to an end any debates about what family life should look like in the twenty-first century.

The ever more loving nurture of infant brains is offered up as the solution to what is perceived to be the root dysfunction of modern society; the dislocation of human beings from one another. In this respect, we can see that neuroparenting provides metaphors for understanding the relationship between humans which are particularly expressive of contemporary anxieties about the constitution of social bonds. In other historical periods, the fundamental questions of human existence have been explored through philosophy, religion, the arts or politics; today there is increasing recourse to neuroscience as a source of answers and these other domains of human thought are often re-explained as the products neurobiological traits (Tallis 2011; Thornton 2011a, b). Neuroparenting brings together two tendencies in contemporary thought: the turn to the brain as a source of universal, transhistorical truths about what it means to be human and the turn to children and babies as moral pivots to anchor us in the search for rules of behaviour. The idea that the naturalness of babies offers an ideological and emotional anchor in times where many other social relationships are being recast in more fluid, contingent terms has been argued by other scholars (see Beck and Beck-Gernsheim 1995; Gillis 1997; Parton 2006). As Stearns puts it, '(T)he baby has become the guardian of stability in an uncertain life' (Stearns, 2003, p. 425).

Hiding Behind Babies' Brains

It is the contention of this book that the turn towards the infant brain is an evasive way of addressing some vitally important questions. This is an abdication by adult society of its responsibility for deciding how children should be socialised. Adults might be said to be hiding behind children in an attempt to create rules for life without actually discussing the basis for those rules. The conversation which needs to happen, about the raising of future citizens, has to happen amongst adult citizens, not through 'baby talk'. We cannot look to the neurobiology of infants to create society in the way we wish it to be made, not least because humans with the same neurobiology have organised themselves to address the task of child-rearing in a huge variety of ways over different contexts of time and space. What we will see throughout the advocacy of neuroparenting is an avoidance of a democratic discussion about crucial issues concerning families, adults and children and an unhelpful attempt to draw on the reassurances of the non-human, natural world of 'brains' to bring in regulations and admonitions from above rather than policies which genuinely connect with people's needs.

Many academics and thinkers have expressed concern about the turn towards the brain in contemporary thinking. This book engages with some of this neurocritical work, but a key finding of our research is that concern for a parenting deficit long predates neuroscience. While we need to grasp the specific purchase that neuroscience-based claims-making has on contemporary thinking, as far as this book is concerned, this task is undertaken in order that we can better understand the broader context of ideas, arguments and actions by which the relationship between families and the state is being reconstructed. This book is not hostile to science or to neuroscience. Anyone who has experienced a neurological disorder at first, second or even third hand will know that increasing the scientific understanding of the brain is of vital importance. But they will also be only too aware of the pretty rudimentary nature of current knowledge and its limited translation into effective medical treatment for many distressing neurological symptoms. It is therefore often difficult to square this relatively primitive state of neuromastery in the medical field with the fantastical claims being made about what 'we now know' about the neurological mediations of human relationships.

In the subsequent chapters, we will first look in more detail at the claims made in the name of neuroscience and parenting. We will then discuss whether science and nature can tell us how to raise our children. The fourth chapter sets out the recent history of the politicisation of 'the early years' of life, before Chap. 5 moves on to consider the consequences of neuroparenting. The concluding chapter warns of the unintended consequences of the attempt to shore up the family by intervening earlier, deeper and universally into the relationship between parents and their children.

References

Allen, G. (2011a). *Early intervention: The next steps*. London: Cabinet Office.
Allen, G. (2011b). *Early intervention: Smart investment, massive savings*. London: Cabinet Office.
Apple, R. D. (1995). Constructing mothers: Scientific motherhood in the nineteenth and twentieth centuries. *Social History of Medicine, 8*(2), 161–178.
Apple, R. (2006). *Perfect motherhood: Science and childrearing in America*. New Brunswick/London: Rutgers University Press.
Beck, U., & Beck-Gernsheim, E. (1995). *The normal chaos of love*. Oxford: Polity Press.

Berger, B., & Berger, P. (1983). *The war over the family: Capturing the middle ground*. New York: Anchor Press/Doubleday.
Cameron, D. (2016). Prime Minister's speech on life chances. https://www.gov.uk/government/speeches/prime-ministers-speech-on-life-chances. Accessed 5 Feb 2016.
Clabough, E. (2016). Neuroparent. Website, http://www.neuroparent.org/. Accessed 12 Jan 2016.
Couchman, G. (1983). Parenting: An informal survey. *American Speech, 58*(3), 285–288.
Daly, M. (2013). Parenting support policies in Europe. *Families Relationships and Societies, 2*(2), 159–174.
Davies, S. (2013). *The '1001 critical days manifesto: The importance of the conception to age two period'*, foreword.
Department of Health (DH). (2011). *Preparation for birth and beyond a resource pack for leaders of community groups and leaders*. London: DH.
Ehrenreich, B., & English, D. (1979). *For her own good: 150 years of the experts' advice to women*. London: Pluto Press.
Evening Standard. (2009). Prince Charles's day on the other side of the tracks, Friday 11 September.
Faircloth, C. (2013). *Militant lactivism? Infant feeding and maternal accountability in the UK and France*. Oxford/New York: Berghahn Books.
Furedi, F. (2001). *Paranoid parenting: Abandon your anxieties and be a good parent*. London: Allen Lane.
Furedi, F. (2008). *Paranoid parenting: Why ignoring the experts may be best for your child* (2nd ed.). London/New York: Continuum.
Gillis, J. R. (1997). *A world of their own making: Myth, ritual, and the quest for family values*. Cambridge, MA: Harvard University Press.
Gillies, V. (2011). From function to competence: Engaging with the new politics of family. *Sociological Research Online, 16*(4), 11. http://www.socresonline.org.uk/16/4/11.html
Hardyment, C. (1995). *Perfect parents: Baby-care advice past and present*. Oxford: Oxford University Press.
Hays, S. (1996). *The cultural contradictions of motherhood*. New Haven/London: Yale University Press.
Hendrick, H. (1997). *Children, childhood and English society 1880–1990*. Cambridge: Cambridge University Press.
Hulbert, A. (2004). *Raising America, experts, parents, and a century of advice about children*. New York: Vintage.
Lee, E. (2016, January 14). Sorry Cameron, but parents don't want your parenting classes. Spiked-online. http://www.spiked-online.com/newsite/article/sorry-cameron-but-parents-dont-want-parenting-classes/17805#.Vsmtq5OLQ6g
Lee, E., Macvarish, J., & Bristow, J. (2010). Editorial: Risk, health and parenting culture. *Health Risk and Society, 12*(4), 293–300.

Lee, E., Lowe, P., & Macvarish, J. (2014a). The uses and abuses of biology: Neuroscience, parenting and family policy in Britain. A 'key findings' report. http://blogs.kent.ac.uk/parentingculturestudies/files/2014/03/UAB-Key-Findings-Report.pdf

Lee, E., Bristow, J., Faircloth, C., & Macvarish, J. (2014b). *Parenting culture studies*. Basingstoke: Palgrave Macmillan.

Lewis, J. (2011). Parenting programmes in England: Policy development and implementation issues, 2005–2010. *Journal of Social Welfare and Family Law, 33*(2), 107–21.

Loughton, T. (2015, March). Foreword to *Building Great Britons*. 1001 Critical Days.

Macvarish, J. (2014). Babies' brains and parenting policy: The insensitive mother, Essay 3. In E. Lee, J. Bristow, C. Faircloth, & J. Macvarish (Eds.), *Parenting culture studies*. London: Palgrave Macmillan.

Macvarish, J., Lee, E., & Lowe, P. (2014). The 'first three years' movement and the infant brain: A review of critiques. *Sociology Compass, 8*(6), 792–804.

Macvarish, J., Lee, E., & Lowe, P. (2015). Neuroscience and family policy: What becomes of the parent? *Critical Social Policy, 35*(2), 248–269.

Orr, D. (2009, January 3). Colourful character: Camila Bathmanghelidjh on her unique approach to charity work. *The Independent*.

Parton, N. (2006). *Safeguarding childhood: Early intervention and surveillance in a late modern society*. Basingstoke: Palgrave Macmillan.

Prince of Wales. (2000). A royal view: BBC Reith lecture, *BBC News Online*, http://news.bbc.co.uk/hi/english/static/events/reith_2000/lecture6.stm. Accessed 5 Jan 2016.

Richardson, H. (2014, April 4). Parenting scheme dubbed a 'flop' by Labour., *BBC News Online*. http://www.bbc.co.uk/news/education-26875470. Accessed, 28 Jan 2016.

Sears, W., & Sears, M. (2001). *The attachment parenting book: A commonsense guide to understanding and nurturing your baby*. London: Little, Brown and Company.

Smith, R. (2010). Total parenting. *Educational Theory, 60*(3), 357–369.

Stearns, P. (2003). *Anxious parents: A history of modern childrearing in America*. New York/London: New York University Press.

Tallis, R. (2011). *Aping mankind: Neuromania, Darwinitis and the misrepresentation of humanity*. Durham: Acumen.

Thornton, D. J. (2011a). Neuroscience, affect and the entrepreneurialization of mother-hood. *Communication and Critical/Cultural Studies, 8*(4), 399–424.

Thornton, D. J. (2011b). *Brain culture: Neuroscience and popular media*. New Brunswick: Rutgers.

Tyler, Baroness of Enfield. (2015, March 5). Foreword to *The parliamentary inquiry into parenting and social mobility enhancing parenting support across the UK*. Family and Daycare Trust.

CHAPTER 2

The Claims of Neuroparenting

Abstract Neuroparenting advocates have translated a few foundational scientific facts about the particular features of human brain development into pseudo-scientific metaphors and 'killer facts' to be deployed in the political argument for early intervention and parent training. The infant brain is constructed as simultaneously 'wondrous', relative to older brains, and 'vulnerable' to toxic substances, toxic technology, toxic environments, toxic stress and ultimately, toxic parents. The toxic metaphor conveys the heightened sense of infant vulnerability, the requirement of parents (mothers in particular) to safeguard their babies from these risks and the profound fear that human socialisation is fundamentally threatening to infant development. Family life, where socialisation is narrowly understood to happen, is therefore pathologised.

Keywords Neuroparenting: science • Neuroscience • Neuroscientism • Scientism • Brain • Metaphor • Claims-making • Social construction of the child • Risk • Child development

Towards the end of the 1990s, declared by US and other governments to be 'the decade of the brain', the philosopher of science John Bruer critically reviewed the claims being made about the infant brain by an increasingly prominent group of policy-actors who were demanding a redirection of educational and social policy attention towards infancy. This new argument and its proponents were subsequently labelled 'the first three years movement' by the US academic, Davi Johnson Thornton (2011) because they argued that neuroscience now proved that state action during the years 0–3 was more effective than any in the later stages of childhood or adult life. Bruer identified three foundational statements about the nature of infant neurobiological development, which underpinned what he came to call 'the myth of the first three years' in his book of the same name (1999):

1. There is a period of rapid synaptic growth or synaptogenesis (the creation of connections between neurons) in the early years, which is unmatched in speed or scale during later periods of human life.
2. There are 'critical' or 'sensitive' periods for particular aspects of brain development in the early years, during which development is dependent on, or expectant of, certain environmental experiences.
3. The brain requires 'enriched environments' or 'stimulation' in the earlier years to develop functionally.

Professor Bruer then traced these core claims back to the scientific research from which they had been constructed. His review of the original research findings found that while the three postulates above are descriptive of some specific aspects of neurological development, they are not generalisable into universal principles of brain growth or totalising theories of human development. In a later collaboration, published as 'Critical Thinking About Critical Periods' (2001), Bruer worked with scientists and educationalists to assess in greater detail, research in the field of developmental neurobiology, bringing together findings from the study of visual development, social and emotional development (including attachment) and language acquisition, to evaluate the argument made by the first three years movement that 'the first years last for ever' and are therefore deserving of policy priority. What Bruer and his colleagues found was that the scientific evidence merited far more modest conclusions about the long-term significance of early brain development than those promulgated in public discourse by neuroparenting advocates. He argued forcefully in his earlier work, published at the height of brain-claiming in the USA, that 'we do not have a revolutionary, brain-based action agenda for child development', hence he gave the book the provocative title, 'The Myth of the First Three Years', and warned that 'looking through this mythical lens gives us a highly distorted view of children, parents, and early childhood policy' (Bruer 1999, p. 25). There are good reasons, therefore, to question the statement that 'the first years last for ever' and to posit that the argument that policy needs to focus primarily on the years 0–3 is an ideological and political one, rather than one that is supported by scientific evidence.

'KILLER FACTS'

The nature of the scientific method is that claims to truth will be continually tested, developed and probably eventually overturned. Scientific findings in the field of biology are specific to particular processes and mechanisms, they do not give rise to overarching theories of 'the body' and they certainly do not form a basis for extrapolating to rules of how humans ought to live. To claim that 'we now know' how babies should be cared for because 'the science says' is therefore fundamentally unscientific. What neuroparenting has done is to turn specific scientific findings into much broader principles that are said to describe early development as a whole. These claims about the brain, which are not 'evidence-based', instead become metaphors. The first three years movement is built on the dramatising of these metaphors, turning them into 'killer facts' (Bowen et al. 2009), in order to make a political case for early intervention policies. These highly emotive claims are used as warnings to society that babies are routinely at risk from parental behaviour and therefore family life needs to be opened up to the protective intervention of government.

The process through which these killer facts have been constructed becomes very clear when we look at the work of Professor Jack Shonkoff, probably the best-known figure in the first three years movement (he was name-checked in David Cameron's 2016 Life Chances speech). His co-authored book, 'From Neurons to Neighbourhoods: The Science of Early Child Development' has achieved global influence and his 'Harvard Center on the Developing Child' (HCDC) is the most often-cited source in neuroparenting claims-making. Shonkoff has described how he worked with a public relations agency to construct 'a core story of development, using simplifying models' (Shonkoff and Bales 2011, p. 17). The agency, The FrameWorks Institute, specialises in 'reframing' public issues and social problems on behalf of campaigns in the non-profit sector, to 'win support, both ideological and financial, for these causes'. This collaboration is the origin of the metaphors 'brain architecture', 'toxic stress' and 'serve and return', which form the core of neuroparenting claims-making today.

By 'framing and re-framing issues', FrameWorks seek to shape the 'way a story is told—its selective use of particular values, symbols, metaphors, and messengers' because, they believe, this 'triggers the shared and durable cultural models that people use to make sense of their world' (Nisbet 2011). FrameWorks' engagement with Jack Shonkoff and his colleagues in the cause of early intervention was aimed at challenging a 'dominant cultural model' which they describe as the 'family bubble' (Nisbet 2011). As far as they were concerned, this model was problematic because it relied on the 'idea that for children under age five, development is the responsibility of the parents', meaning that 'people operating from this model will not support policies like subsidized pre-kindergarten programs' (Nisbet 2011). In order to challenge the 'family bubble', FrameWorks wanted to 'activate' another model, based on the idea of 'brain architecture', which establishes 'the idea that from birth to age five, the human brain is developing the foundation upon which all future learning and function will rest, impacting academic performance, employability, and ultimately, the competitiveness of the national workforce' (Nisbet 2011).

What this very candid description demonstrates is that 'the science' is secondary to the policy agenda. The myth of the first three years is, as John Bruer suggests, 'just another rhetorical tool that happens to elicit a strong emotional response in the public' (Bruer 1999, p. 25). We will discuss in Chap. 3 why the recourse to science has rhetorical appeal, but in this chapter we will demonstrate in more detail how 'the science' of the first three years movement operates as a set of translational metaphors, precisely as intended.

Two Constructions of the Brain

In much of the first three years movement literature, claims are made about the brain with no reference to supporting evidence. Often there is merely the deployment of neuro-buzzwords, which invoke the key brain facts outlined at the start of this chapter. Looked at thematically, we can see how the core brain claims give rise to two broader descriptions of the brain; they are (a) the wondrous brain and (b) the vulnerable brain.

The Wondrous Brain

When babies' brains are invoked by neuroparenting advocates, they are usually talked of in reverential terms. In particular, claims about the speed and scale of neural development in the earliest months and years are used to inspire wonder and awe. A twitter post from the UK's 1001 Critical Days campaign contains a photograph of a newborn baby's head, cradled by a mother's hands, with the following exclamatory strapline:

> From birth to 18 months, it has been calculated that connections in the brain are created at a rate of a million per second! The earliest experiences shape a baby's brain development, and have a lifelong impact on that baby's mental and emotional health.

The infant brain is not just 'amazing', constituted of mind-bogglingly large numbers of 'connections', it is also often positioned as being more wondrous than the adult brain. An information pack for National Health Service (NHS) maternity staff contains the claim, 'Amazing growth takes place in infancy – it takes just seven minutes for the synapses of each neuron to form. By three years of age there are trillions of connections – twice as many as an adult has' (DH 2011). The same theme is echoed by the British Member of Parliament (MP), Graham Allen, a significant early disseminator of neuroparenting in the United Kingdom (UK), in his report, 'Early Intervention: The Next Steps':

> The early years are far and away the greatest period of growth in the human brain. It has been estimated that the connections or synapses in a baby's brain grow 20-fold, from having perhaps 10 trillion at birth to 200 trillion at age 3. (Allen 2011, p. 6)

The wondrous brain trope has been a consistent presence in the first three years movement since the late 1990s. Describing the formation of synaptical connections as 'miracles of the human body', which 'you have to multiply by trillions' to 'understand their power', this information pack for parent educators on the 'The First Years Last Forever' programme, produced by the University of Wisconsin back in 1999, also exemplified the mind-boggling brain facts tendency: 'We are born with over 100 billion brain cells or neurons; we will not grow more. That's about ten times the number of stars in the entire Milky Way and twenty times the number of people on the planet' (University of Wisconsin 1999).

The sense of awe at infant development has been identified as arising in the 1970s, two decades in advance of neuroscience coming to prominence. According to the psychologist Professor Erica Burman, it was at this time that claims from developmental psychology began to describe the human infant as more 'competent' than previously believed. The historian Elizabeth Hulbert similarly identifies the late 1970s and early 1980s as 'the Golden Age' of infant research (2004, p. 300), when the idea came to prevail in psychology and beyond, that the development of the human infant was constituted of a far more complex interrelationship between the innate and the experiential than was previously thought. In 1974, the psychologist Lawrence Joseph Stone and colleagues published the book, 'The Competent Infant', articulating the new theme which became typical of the age.

In the early 1980s, the popular US paediatrician Dr T. Berry Brazelton rewrote his 1969 book 'Infants and Mothers: Differences in Development', constructing the baby as interactive and born competent (Hulbert 2004, p. 310). An article published in *The Atlantic* at the time reflected on this shift in the view of babies:

> In the past twenty years, and dramatically in the past ten, the 'can't-do' baby that Spock described has been eclipsed by a 'can-do' baby – a baby so attuned and responsive to his environment that, even in the uterus, he is reacting to voices, to light, and, perhaps, to his mother's moods. This 'new' baby is activated not only by internal pain and appetite but by language and smiles and particular people. The operative word, in descriptions of this baby, is 'competence.' (Quinn 1982)

The article cites comments by Brazelton about the current 'burst of knowledge about infant competence' and goes on to report his description of past attitudes in paediatrics when he started out in the 1950s:

> we were blaming parents for everything that happened to babies. And that was a counterproductive stance. Parents are not responsible for everything that happens to babies, because the baby is already having a pretty strong effect on his own future. (Quinn 1982)

The new discoveries from developmental psychology seemed to offer reassurance to parents that their baby would be naturally prone to normal development and everything would turn out alright if they just followed the baby's lead. We might expect the discovery of the competent infant to be a 'good news story', with the early years potentially understood as a time of infinite possibilities and an impressive infant drive to develop the uniquely sophisticated evolutionary achievement represented by the human brain. Brazelton claimed that he was now able to reassure parents, who frequently asked him, 'How do I know I'm doing the right thing?' with the advice, 'Watch the baby, he'll tell you.' But even in Brazelton's remarks, as well as the 'wonder' at the newly discovered, 'competent' infant, we can also see evidence of the trope we will discuss next, that of the vulnerable infant brain, in Brazelton's words:

> All of us who are interested in preserving the family as an optimal source of important experience for the vulnerable developing infant must see our goals clearly. We must be careful to provide environmental supports that reinforce the strength and rewards of reciprocal affective ties within the family! (Quinn 1982)

It is evident from Brazelton's comments that he has underlying concerns about the state of the family, in particular about the strength of the parent–child bond. He talks of 'preserving' the 'affective ties within the family' and cautions that the use of day care threatens family bonds (Quinn 1982). At a time when women were entering the workforce in greater numbers, it seems with hindsight that Brazelton was almost 'marketing' the baby to the mother as worthy of a semi-professionalised interest. The mother becomes more like an expert and experimenter in child development in the way she can interact with her baby in daily life. By emphasising the baby's previously unknown capacities, the status of motherhood can be put onto a footing where it can compete with the stimulation and status of a career. This new, psychologised romanticisation of the wondrous infant was shaped as much in response to the profound social changes of the 1970s and 1980s in the construction of gender, as informed by research from the laboratory.

We can see then, that the view of the infant as 'amazing' precedes the rise of neuroscience in the 1990s and the contemporary focus on the brain. What is also evident is that with the rise of the competent infant, there was a shift in the relative positions of baby and parent. Whereas newborn babies had been understood as relatively simple in both needs and capacity, the competent infant is rendered more interesting and engaging, but also more needy and more difficult to raise. The article's author, Susan Quinn, concludes that 'the baby has replaced the books as the ultimate authority' (Quinn 1982); it is the child psychologist who has revealed this new truth about babies' competence to the parent. The child development expert is the interpreter of the baby's attempts at communication and must train the parent to be cognisant of its needs. The implication is that we have previously misunderstood the human infant, thereby failing to sensitively meet their needs and missing opportunities to develop their full potential. The threat is that we will continue to be out of synch with babies, unless we listen to the likes of T. Berry Brazelton. The parent is therefore demoted relative to both the baby and the parenting expert.

The Vulnerable Brain

In today's neuroparenting discourse, the awe-inspiring infant brain is always a preface to another type of claim, the 'vulnerability trope'. Killer facts of natural development are immediately followed by a warning; of those 'trillions of connections', 'only those that are used regularly will remain' (DH 2011). And so, a natural and necessary process of 'synaptic pruning' is talked of with a sense of regret and the threat of lost opportunities. In much of the neuro-rhetoric, the brain is at its best in the earliest years of life but it is also at its most vulnerable to negative environmental influences. The encouraging and reassuring discovery of human brain 'plasticity' is therefore interpreted as a source of vulnerability, not resilience.

Toxic Substances

The dominant way in which the vulnerability of the infant brain to external influences is articulated is through the metaphor of toxicity. Most literally, there is the presence of toxic substances, consumed by the pregnant mother and talked of as being transmitted to the foetus in utero, through the placenta. The most prominent is the concern about the impact mothers drinking alcohol may have on foetal brain formation.

Historians and sociologists have traced how concern with maternal alcohol consumption has moved from being the preserve of very small campaign groups to being an officially promoted tenet of the maternal advice scaffolding (Armstrong 2003; Golden 2005; Lee et al. 2014). Despite the absence of causal evidence of harm in all but the most extreme cases of alcoholism, in the UK, maternal health policy has placed an increasing emphasis on total abstention as the only safe option in pregnancy (Lowe and Lee 2010). The threat of Fetal Alcohol Syndrome and Fetal Alcohol Spectrum Disorder has been amplified considerably in the past ten years, based on active lobbying around claims of the brain-damaging effects of alcohol consumption on the vulnerable foetus (Lee et al. 2014; Lowe and Lee 2010; Lowe et al. 2010). In a recent parliamentary debate, one advocate of the 1001 Critical Days campaign spoke dramatically of the 'carnage' being wreaked on British infants by maternal drinking, indicating that the highly moralised question of pregnant women's behaviour is an important part of the first three years movement agenda in the UK.

A visceral fear of producing an intellectually impaired and physically deformed child does seem to have taken a hold on pregnant women. This soon-to-be mother of three sought reassurance, early one Sunday morning, from an online forum:

> Sun 13-Sep-15 07:36:44 This is dc3 [third child]. When pg [pregnant] with dc2 [second child] advice was that there was no problem with low consumption of alcohol. I still didn't drink much in that pregnancy maybe on half a dozen occasions 1 or 2 drinks max. When I found out I was pregnant this time I was on holiday I continued to have a very small glass of cider 2% alcohol most nights for the following week. Thinking that the alcohol content was so low and it was a small amount. Then since then I've probably had 4/5 occasions where I've drunk a glass (sometimes a large glass) of red wine with a meal. My attention has now been drawn to guidelines that state no alcohol should be consumed in pregnancy. I am beside myself with worry. I'm struggling to gain perspective on this. Can I get your opinions.

The following day, the worried mother returns to the forum:

> Well I saw the midwife today. She didn't really set my mind at ease. She said I wouldn't know if it would have had any effect until they have developmental check by the health visitor at e.g. 2 years old ☹. The rational side of me says that I haven't consumed anything excessive and that the amount I've had would not have had an effect on the baby. But I'm a worrier by nature so I'll continue to worry and won't drink anything else now for the remainder of the pregnancy. (Mumsnet 2015)

This is an experienced mother of two children, about to have her third, whose existing knowledge and experience is thrown up in the air by new medical advice, disseminated by public health campaigns and reinforced by midwives, that the foetal brain is at risk from any alcohol consumption at all during pregnancy, despite no new evidence of harm associated with very moderate drinking such as hers.

After birth, concern about neurological risks moves from drink consumed by the mother to the food ingested directly by the infant, most obviously in the debate over the relative developmental benefits of breast milk or formula milk. There are persistent claims that breast milk impacts positively on intelligence (see Wolf 2011, for a critical evaluation and also Blum 1999), but also preventatively on developmental disorders (Norton 2015). One UK newspaper reported, 'Breastfeeding your baby could protect them from autism', and went on to claim that 'Mothers who do not breastfeed their babies could be putting them at increased risk of autism' (Sykes 2015). However, on further investigation of the same story in another news source, it seems that the researchers responsible for the study made no such claims; 'the authors and other experts stressed that the study offers no evidence that breast-feeding ultimately affects a child's odds of developing autism, or that it lessens the severity of autism symptoms' (medicalxpress 2015).

Given that that there are only two choices when it comes to feeding young babies, breast milk or formula milk, if 'breast is best', then formula milk is, by implication, second best at least, and harmful at worst in terms of brain development. The implication is that formula feeding is 'toxic' or at least, not protective of cognitive and behavioural development. The negative consequences of this fear-mongering about formula milk for new mothers' confidence in their own decision-making have now become very evident through academic research (Lee 2007a, b, 2011).

Toxic Technology
Children's brains are also said to be at risk from new technology in the form of screens and mobile phones (Richardson 2012). Sue Palmer, the author of 'Toxic Childhood: How the modern world is damaging our children and what we can do about it' (2007), claims that 'screen saturation' is implicated in attention deficit disorder, dyslexia and autism (Palmer 2010). The brain warnings of another prominent screen-denouncer, Aric Sigman, were reported in the *Daily Mail* with the headline, 'TV-addict children "are harming their brains": Youngsters' screen addiction could cause similar changes to those seen in alcoholics' (Norton 2014), while neuroscientist Susan Greenfield has been criticised by others in her field for claiming that digital media pose a risk to brain development (Bishop 2014a). In a further twist on the toxic screens theme, a *Time* magazine article reported that mothers 'distracted' by their mobile phones may fail to interact responsively with their infants, resulting in neurological dam-

age, failing to mention, however, that this statement of fact was derived from an experiment with rats. Unsurprisingly, the mother rats were not distracted from the care of their pups by mobile phones but by the frantic search for straw bedding, of which they had been initially deprived, but this didn't stop one of the researchers leaping to human claims-making:

> What we are proposing is that there is a sensitive period in which maternal care needs to provide consistent patterns and sequences of behavior so the baby's brain can perceive them to develop normally emotionally. The predictability of maternal care seems to engage the pleasure system, and the pleasure system needs to be engaged so the neurons involved will fire together and then will wire together. (Park 2016)

There is a strong anti-modern theme expressed in these toxic threats: pregnant women enjoying a drink, mothers making use of infant formula or using digital technology to entertain themselves or their children are all possible either because of changes in women's position in the world or advances in technology. There is a suggestion that mothers should be encouraged to engage in more 'natural' maternal behaviour (like rats?) to secure their child's normal development (an idea we will explore further in Chap. 3).

Toxic Environments
The latest book by influential American sociologist Robert D. Putnam (name-checked as 'Bob' Putnam by David Cameron in his 2016 Life Chances speech) exemplifies the way in which pseudo-scientific claims-making has become part of a mainstream political agenda which merges concerns about social and moral disorder with concerns about social justice. 'Our Kids: The American Dream in Crisis' initially sets out the problem of worsening inequality and stalled social mobility in twenty-first-century America as the result of de-industrialisation and economic stagnation. However, by his third chapter, Putnam turns to poor parenting as the more significant cause of contemporary social problems. Borrowing almost exclusively from Jack Shonkoff's work, Putnam claims that 'we now know' how 'young children's early experiences and socioeconomic environment influence their neurobiological development, and how, in turn, early neurobiological development influences their later lives' (Putnam 2015, p. 109). What is an understandable moral or political objection to poverty, inequality and related social problems segues into a claim that they are 'wrong' because they create biological dysfunction.

This theme of the 'social toxicity' of inequality is a powerful one at the heart of the first three years movement and it has become increasingly mainstream in recent years. James Garbarino, of the Family Life Development Center at Cornell University, demonstrates the translation of science-derived metaphors of toxicity into calls for policy action:

> What I mean by the term socially toxic environment is that the social world of children, the social context in which they grow up, has become poisonous to their development. I offer this term as a parallel to the environmental movement's analysis regarding physical toxicity as a threat to human well being and survival…But what are the social equivalents to lead and smoke in the air, PCBs in the water, and pesticides in the food chain? I think some social equivalents include violence, poverty and other economic pressures on parents and their children. They include disruption of family relationships and other trauma, despair, depression, paranoia, nastiness and alienation – all contaminants which demoralize families and communities. These are the forces in the land that contaminate the environment of children and youth. These are the elements of social toxicity…Social life is more risky now than it was just 40 years ago; the level of social and cultural poison is higher. (Garbarino 1998)

Neuroscience is thus deployed not only to prove that social inequalities are harmful to individuals, but that this harm is itself the cause of the problem. (In Chap. 3 we will discuss further the biologisation of social and moral problems.) Of course, this ends up in a cyclical theory of causation which has antecedents in much earlier theories of cycles of deprivation or self-perpetuating underclass moral degeneracy (Welshman 2008; Macvarish 2014). Today such arguments locate the cause of, and the solution to, the problems of deprivation in poorer neighbourhoods within the parental nurture of children's brains. The idea that such problems might stem from economic stagnation is abandoned and poverty is reworked as a problem generated by the poor quality parenting carried out by poor people.

Conversely, according to neuroparenting and the first three years movement, 'enriched environments' are created by positive parental action, consciously stimulating their babies, providing educational and extra-curricular support for their school-aged children: the 'Tiger Moms' praised by David Cameron in his Life Chances speech (referencing Amy Chua's 2011 book, Battle Hymn of the Tiger Mother). The time- and resource-intensive practices of a section of the middle class are naturalised as 'stimulating' brain growth rather than understood as being the particular lifestyle made possible by being better-paid, better-educated parents with a particular anxiety to fend off downward mobility in their offspring (Hays 1996; Lareau 2003). The idea that the infant brain requires what Lareau labelled 'concerted cultivation' (2003) by caregivers in order to achieve normal functioning has become entrenched in policy.

Much of this claims-making can be traced back to animal studies. Studies which suggest that rats raised in 'isolated' environments, devoid of stimulation, develop smaller brains (or some smaller parts to their brains) than rats raised in environments which are 'complex', with many sources of stimulation, have been used to infer that 'deprived' (poor) human environments must also be negative for brain growth, whereas 'enriched' (wealthier) environments have positive effects (Bruer 1999, p. 145). Even if rat brains and human brains are comparable at some very basic level, common sense should make us question whether struggling to get by in an economically deprived environment can really be described as 'under-stimulating'. Nevertheless, the biological claim that 'enriched' environments increase brain size is then mapped onto the differential educational outcomes of poor children relative to their wealthier peers, thus rooting class differences in educational achievement within the brain and laying the blame with poor parents who have failed to provide sufficient stimulation in the early years of the child's life. The solution to economic stagnation, entrenched inequality and stalled social mobility therefore becomes a matter of training parents to take responsibility for these huge structural problems by changing the way they intimately interact with their infants.

Toxic Parents
Another much-cited cornerstone of the idea that there is a causal relationship between poor parenting and poor child outcomes is the so-called 'thirty millions words' claim (again, mentioned by Cameron in his 2016 'Life Chances' speech) that the poorest child will hear 30 million more words spoken in the family home during the pre-school years than the wealthiest child. The claim is based on a 1995 study of just 42 American infants aged seven months to three years, representing four social income groups (high, middle, working class and on welfare). The research team, led by Betty Hart and Todd R. Risley, observed the children in their homes for one hour a month, counting the number of words spoken in the child's presence during their visit. From this, they extrapolated the 30 million words differential between the 13 highest status children and the 6 children whose families

were on welfare. Their report was headlined in dramatic terms, 'the early catastrophe' and has since been turned into a global campaign for parental behaviour change (Hart and Risley, 2003). The findings are repeatedly used to 'prove' that class differentials in early educational outcomes are reducible to the number of words parents say to their babies.

Neuroparenting social entrepreneur Professor Dana Suskind has turned Hart and Risley's attention-grabbing claim into a book, 'Thirty Million Words: Building a child's brain', and a copyrighted intervention, the 'Thirty Million Words Initiative'. Suskind is a paediatrician specialising in cochlear implant surgery but her project is not aimed at helping deaf children and their families, but at improving parents in general, especially poor ones. New mothers are recruited in maternity wards by trainers who aim to teach them how to 'enhance their home language environment in order to optimize their child's brain development and, therefore, his or her ability to learn' (Suskind 2016). However, Suskind says that she is not really interested in language, she is interested in the 'quality' of parental care and admits that '(W)e're using the lever of parent talk to get into the parent–child relationship' (Neufeld 2015).

The theme of getting parents to talk to young infants has been translated into other projects too. The 'Too Small to Fail' programme gives out baby-gros and t-shirts via paediatric clinics and child care programmes with messages like 'Let's Talk About Colors' as conversation-starting prompts to parents. Parents might also receive text messages containing 'talking reminders and tips'. The programme trains lower class parents, in the home, to 'tune in', 'talk more' and 'take turns' with their pre-school children in order 'to close the achievement gap between poor families and better off families'. Another programme gives out devices, pinned to a baby's clothing, which count the number of words adults say to them in a day and how many chances they get to respond. Targets can then be set towards which parents 'work' (Trevelyan 2014). Such interventions recast family communication in instrumental terms as measurable and improvable. Parental conversation is redefined as 'input', while the child's development is interpreted as an accurate embodiment of the quality and quantity of the parents' nurturing skills.

Critical voices have raised concerns about the claim that parental input determines language development. A British developmental psychologist who specialises in language development, sceptical of claims that parents should only use 'parent-facing' pushchairs or strollers so that baby and parent can communicate face-to-face at all times, investigated the evidence of a link between infant language acquisition and parental talk and found that, 'attractive as the proposal may be, there is as yet no evidence that child language learning difficulties are caused by lack of parental talk' (Smith 2015). An epidemiological study looking at factors associated with late language emergence (LLE) in toddlers in Australia concluded that:

> Risk for LLE at 24 months was not associated with particular strata of parental educational levels, socioeconomic resources, parental mental health, parenting practices, or family functioning. Significant predictors included familial history of LLE, male gender, and early neurobiological growth. This study concluded that neurobiological factors and genes were important in determining which children had language difficulties. (Zubrick et al. 2007)

Similarly, Dorothy Bishop, neuroscientist and committed critic of dubious neuro-claims-making, argues that genetically determined neurobiology is far more significant than parental input when it comes to language acquisition. She cites studies with children of deaf parents which found that such children can learn to speak because of their exposure to adults outside the home and to language on the television (Bishop 2014b). Psychologist and speech and language therapist Professor Courtenay Frazer Norbury argues that the claim that parents are responsible for language development and the generalised early intervention approach to encourage parental talk means that children who really need specialist support slip through the net, especially those whose problems become apparent only after the age of 3 (Norbury 2015).

Yet despite the lack of evidence of a causal, neurobiological relationship between the amount of parental speech and longer-term child outcomes, in the UK, Thirty Million Words is increasingly mentioned by first three years advocates and translated into many extravagant claims about the need to improve parental communication. David Cameron called it a 'staggering statistic', claiming that '(T)he more words children heard, the higher their IQ, and the better they did in school down the track' and concluding that 'mums and dads literally build babies' brains'. All of this based on a study of 42 children, 6 of whom allegedly heard fewer words than 13 others, conducted by educational early intervention activists, with no connection to brain science.

Toxic Stress

Another very popular neuroconcept that has been widely adopted by first three years advocates is the idea of 'toxic stress'. We do not have space here to adequately reflect the extent of claims-making in this area, but it follows the same pattern as other neuroparenting claims: reliance on animal studies; merging the uterine environment with the family home; the speculative construction of causal relationships, and the extension of claims from extreme cases to everyday parenting. Toxic stress is another claim emanating from the Harvard Center on the Developing Child. To summarise, the substance of the toxic stress claim is that:

- 'Toxic stress' is very damaging to the infant brain, it is as bad, perhaps even worse, than neglect. This stress is transmitted to the child from the parent, *in utero* and postnatally, by parental mood and behaviour.
- The experience of stress in infancy impairs the 'executive functions' of the brain, making it more difficult for the individual to make decisions in later life.

In 'Our Kids: The American Dream in Crisis', Robert Putnam draws on the HCDC's material to make the case that 'toxic stress' is caused by multiple factors; 'unstable and consistently unresponsive caregivers, physical or emotional abuse, parental substance abuse, and lack of affection', claiming that it 'can produce measurable physiological changes in the child that lead to lifelong difficulties in learning, behaviour and both physical and mental health, including depression, alcoholism, obesity and heart disease' (Putnam 2015, p. 112). Putnam is relatively late to the game however, as back in 2011, the American Academy of Paediatrics issued a 'landmark warning' that toxic stress induces lifelong harm. As Ilina Singh outlines, it was claimed that:

> poverty, lack of community resources, lack of education, abuse and neglect, as well as high-stress conditions such as war and famine – create stresses that are literally written into the biological processes of development, penetrating environments from micro (for example, the cellular environment) to macro (for example, home or community environments) with lasting, measurable, heritable physiological and psychological effects. (Singh 2012, p. 311)

While it is sometimes claimed that 'toxic stress' only arises in extreme cases, 'such as placing children in a succession of foster homes or displacement due to economic instability or a natural disaster' (HCDC, toxic stress webpage 2016) very often, the threat is expanded to include everyday experiences, such as parents arguing or babies being left to cry themselves to sleep. British child care guru Penelope Leach warns that the technique of 'controlled crying', whereby parents train babies to get themselves off to sleep by leaving them in their cots for successively longer periods, raises stress levels in the infant to intolerable and harmful levels. Leach says, '(W)e are talking about the release of stress chemicals. The best known of them is cortisol, which is produced under extreme stress' (Richardson 2010). Therefore, what was once an entirely normal practice, leaving babies to 'cry it out', has become talked of as a neurologically treacherous parenting decision, as Leach claims:

> One is not talking about a wakeful baby lying there gurgling, one is talking about a baby that is crying hard and nobody is responding. When that happens, and particularly if it happens over a long period, the brain chemical system releases cortisol and that is very bad for brain development. Some neuroscientists describe it as toxic. (Richardson 2010)

Given that all babies cry at least some of the time and some of them cry an awful lot, despite the efforts of their parents to soothe them, toxic stress must therefore be a potential threat in every family home. In a similar elision of extreme neglect with ordinary infant care, Robert Putnam draws no distinction between the extreme poverty and violence of some US communities and the 'everyday hassles of parenting', amongst which he includes, 'cleaning up after the kids, managing multiple schedules, lack of privacy, and lack of time for self and partner'; parents, he says, 'also have to cope with the ordinary stresses of the rest of life, especially work' (Putnam 2015, p. 130). It would seem that work is as much of a problem as worklessness; both create stressful homes which are threatening to, rather than nurturing of, the vulnerable infant brain.

Pathologising Family Life

What we can see in the examples of toxic threats discussed above is how some problems are invented, some are expanded and others are reconceptualised in biological terms through the borrowing of scientific vocabulary, but they all contribute to a culture in which parents must manage an ever-increasing number of risks (Lee et al. 2010). How are parents to know whether, as far as the foetal brain is concerned, 'stress' connotes the stress of a war zone or parental concerns about the financial consequences of taking maternity leave? Is a 'deprived environment' a cold Romanian orphanage with no toys or pictures, inadequate food and scarce human contact, or is it a family which cannot afford the latest brain-boosting infant products or which struggles to fit in an extra bedtime story? Is a 'stimulating environment' one where older brothers and sisters entertain a baby or only one in which the parent fills the walls with alphabets, timestables and spends time each day, becoming her child's 'first teacher'? Is leaving a baby to cry for hours as 'toxic' as the baby crying for a few minutes while the mother takes a shower? Normal aspects of human life, such as eating and drinking, making conversation or worrying, become pathologised and instrumentalised by their neurobiologisation.

As we will see throughout our consideration of neuroparenting discourse, it can often seem that there is no 'normal' left, as the sensitivity of the young brain to external influences, which is the essence of its 'plasticity', positions the human brain as essentially innocent in its animal or natural state but vulnerable to corruption by its humanising socialisation. This 'use and abuse' of scientific concepts matters for science and it matters for public debate. Science is degraded by its misuse and public debate is degraded by advocates who hide behind pseudo-scientific metaphors, even if they have the best intentions. The paradigms by which we understand children and parents really matter and we should interrogate the arguments used to remould them. Writing critically of developmental psychology, Professor Erica Burman draws out the expansive and very serious consequences of the way in which understandings of the child are put into action:

> on what basis do law courts arrive at an understanding of what constitutes a child's 'best interest'? Or, when is a child deemed to have sufficient understanding to be legally responsible for their actions? What underlies an education welfare officer's opinion that a child's 'social and emotional needs' will be better catered for outside mainstream school? What criteria do adoption agencies use in evaluating whether or not adoption is likely to be successful? What intellectual resources and expertise do legal and welfare professionals turn to when they seek to determine children's competence to participate in decision-making? These are some of the ways in which developmental

psychology reverberates far beyond the theory or the experimental laboratory, as well as beyond the pages of child advice magazines and toyshops. (Burman 2007, p. 9)

So when neuroparenting advocates set out, behind the scenes in the policy-making domain, to shift our understandings of family, privacy, parental responsibility and children's needs—to 'trigger' our 'cultural models' of how the world works in order to make policy seem 'commonsense'—we need a critical response which interrogates their claims, evaluates their political reasoning, explores their interests and considers the consequences (intended and unintended) of the policies they advocate.

What Erica Burman's critique of developmental psychology helps us to realise is that the 'neuro' in 'neuroparenting' is not so significant as it might first appear. The claims of neuroparenting rely more on developmental psychology and behavioural science than on neuroscience itself. As John Bruer also observed, the emphasis on 'the first three years' of a baby's life as crucial to lifelong development draws more on psychiatry and psychology than on 'brain science'. In some ways it can be argued that neuroscience merely adds the glisten of novelty to some fairly long-standing claims. But brain-claiming does have one very significant effect, it promises to provide the material evidence, visible in the biological structure of the brain, of the quality and quantity of parental love and care. Constructing the brain as such gives licence to the advocacy of a particular way of raising children that is anxious, intensive and scrutinised from without, which threatens parents with the prospect of a brain-impaired child who is of their making.

References

Allen, G. (2011). *Early intervention: The next steps*. London: Cabinet Office.
Armstrong, E. M. (2003). *Conceiving risk, bearing responsibility: Fetal alcohol syndrome and the diagnosis of moral disorder*. Baltimore: The John Hopkins University Press.
Bishop, D. (2014a). Why most scientists don't take Susan Greenfield seriously. Blogpost, http://deevybee.blogspot.co.uk/2014/09/why-most-scientists-dont-take-susan.html. Accessed 10 Jan 2016.
Bishop, D. (2014b). Parent talk and child language. Blogpost, http://deevybee.blogspot.co.uk/2014/02/parent-talk-and-child-language.html?m=1. Accessed 10 Jan 2016.

Blum, L. (1999). *At the breast: Ideologies of breastfeeding and motherhood in the contemporary United States*. Boston: Beacon Press.

Bowen, S., Zwi, A., Sainsbury, P., & Whitehead, M. (2009). Killer facts, politics and other influences: What evidence triggered early childhood intervention policies in Australia? *Evidence & Policy, 5*(1), 5–32.

Bruer, J. (1999). *The myth of the first three years: A new understanding of early brain development and lifelong learning*. New York: The Free Press.

Burman, E. (2007). *Deconstructing developmental psychology* (2nd ed.). E.Sussex/New York: Routledge.

Cameron, D. (2016). Prime Minister's speech on life chances. https://www.gov.uk/government/speeches/prime-ministers-speech-on-life-chances. Accessed 5 Feb 2016.

Chua, A. (2011). *Battle hymn of the tiger mother*. London: Penguin.

Department of Health (DH). (2011). *Preparation for birth and beyond a resource pack for leaders of community groups and leaders*. London: DH.

Garbarino, J. (1998). Supporting parents in a socially toxic environment. http://parenthood.library.wisc.edu/Garbarino/Garbarino.html. Accessed 10 Jan 2016.

Golden, J. (2005). *Message in a bottle: The making of fetal alcohol syndrome*. Cambridge/London: Harvard University Press.

Hart, B., & Risley, T. (2003). The early catastrophe: The 30 million word gap by age 3. *American Educator, 27*, 4–9.

Hays, S. (1996). *The cultural contradictions of motherhood*. New Haven/London: Yale University Press.

HCDC. (2016). Harvard Center on the Developing Child, toxic stress response. http://developingchild.harvard.edu/index.php/key_concepts/toxic_stress_response/. Accessed 16 Jan 2016.

Hulbert, A. (2004). *Raising America, experts, parents, and a century of advice about children*. New York: Vintage.

Lareau, A. (2003). *Unequal childhoods: Class, race, and family life*. Berkeley: University of California Press.

Lee, E. (2007a). Health, morality, and infant feeding: British mothers' experiences of formula milk use in the early weeks. *Sociology of Health and Illness, 29*(7), 1075–1090.

Lee, E. (2007b). Infant feeding in risk society. *Health Risk and Society, 9*(3), 295–309.

Lee, E. (2011). Breast-feeding advocacy, risk society and health moralism: A decade's scholarship. *Sociology Compass, 5*(12), 1058–1069.

Lee, E., Macvarish, J., & Bristow, J. (2010). Editorial: Risk, health and parenting culture. *Health Risk and Society, 12*(4), 293–300.

Lee, E., Bristow, J., Faircloth, C., & Macvarish, J. (2014). *Parenting culture studies*. Basingstoke: Palgrave Macmillan.

Lowe, P., & Lee, E. (2010). Advocating alcohol abstinence to pregnant women: Some observations about British policy. *Health, Risk and Society, 12*(4), 301–312.

Lowe, P., Lee, E., & Yardley, L. (2010). Under the influence? The construction of foetal alcohol syndrome in UK newspapers. *Sociological Research Online, 15*(4), 2. http://www.socresonline.org.uk/15/4/2.html

Macvarish, J. (2014). The politics of parenting, Chapter 3. In E. Lee, J. Bristow, C. Faircloth, & J. Macvarish (Eds.), *Parenting culture studies*. London: Palgrave Macmillan.

Mumsnet. (2015). Worries regarding alcohol in pregnancy. Anonymous web post. http://www.mumsnet.com/Talk/pregnancy/2466838-Worries-regarding-alcohol-in-pregnancy, Sunday 13 September. Accessed 10 Jan 2016.

Neufeld, S. (2015). How do you make a baby smart? Word by word, a Chicago project says. http://hechingerreport.org/content/make-baby-smart-word-word-chicago-project-says_18681/. Accessed 10 Jan 2016.

Nisbet, M. (2011). The Frameworks Institute: Changing the conversation about policy problems. http://bigthink.com/age-of-engagement/the-frameworks-institute-changing-the-conversation-about-policy-problems. Accessed 10 Jan 2016.

Norbury, C. F. (2015). Editorial: Early intervention in response to language delays—Is there a danger of putting too many eggs in the wrong basket? *Journal of Child Psychology and Psychiatry, 56*, 835–836.

Norton, J. (2014, July 4). TV addict children "are harming their brains". *Daily Mail.* http://www.dailymail.co.uk/news/article-2680154/TV-addict-children-harming-brains-Youngsters-screen-addiction-cause-similar-changes-seen-alcoholics.html. Accessed 12 Jan 2016.

Norton, A. (2015). Breastfeeding tied to better emotion perception in some infants. http://medicalxpress.com/news/2015-09-breastfeeding-tied-emotion-perception-infants.html. Accessed 12 Jan 2016.

Palmer, S. (2007). *Toxic childhood: How the modern world is damaging our children and what we can do about it.* London: Orion.

Palmer, S. (2010). Screen saturation and child development, online article. http://www.suepalmer.co.uk/modern_childhood_info_the_effects.php. Accessed 10 Jan 2016.

Park, A. (2016, January 6). Cell-phone distracted parenting can have long-term consequences: Study. *Time Magazine*, online article. http://time.com/4168688/cell-phone-distracted-parenting-can-have-long-term-consequences-study/. Accessed 17 Jan 2016.

Putnam, R. (2015). *Our kids: The American dream in crisis.* New York: Simon and Schuster.

Quinn, S. (1982, January). The competence of babies. *The Atlantic.* http://www.theatlantic.com/magazine/archive/1982/01/the-competence-of-babies/305128/. Accessed 7 Jan 2016.

Richardson, H. (2010, April 22). Crying-it-out harms babies' brains. *BBC News Online.* http://news.bbc.co.uk/1/hi/education/8636950.stm. Accessed 12 Jan 2016.

Richardson, H. (2012, October 9). Limit children's screen time, expert urges. *BBC News Online.* http://www.bbc.co.uk/news/education-19870199. Accessed 1 July 2013.

Shonkoff, J. P., & Bales, S. (2011). Science does not speak for itself: Translating child development research for the public and its policymakers. *Child Development, 82*(1), 17–32.

Singh, I. (2012). Human development, nature and nurture: Working beyond the divide. *BioSocieties, 7*(3), 308–321.

Smith, C. (2015). Debunking parenting myths. Blogpost, http://clarrysmith.blogspot.co.uk/2015/01/debunking-parenting-myths-tale-of.html. Accessed 17 Jan 2016.

Suskind, D. (2016). Webpage. http://www.uchicagokidshospital.org/physicians/dana-suskind.html. Accessed 17 Jan 2016.

Sykes, S. (2015, September 14). Breastfeeding your baby could protect them from autism a new study says. *Express.* http://www.express.co.uk/news/uk/605219/Breastfeeding-protect-baby-autism. Accessed 12 Jan 2016.

Thornton, D. J. (2011). Neuroscience, affect and the entrepreneurialization of mother-hood. *Communication and Critical/Cultural Studies,* 8 (4), 399–424.

Trevelyan, L. (2014, March 5). Closing the 'Word Gap' by teaching parents to talk to babies. *BBC News Online,* online article. http://www.bbc.co.uk/news/magazine-26439798. Accessed 12 Jan 2015.

University of Wisconsin. (1999, June). The first years last for ever. *Resource Pack.*

Welshman, J. (2008). The cycle of deprivation: Myths and misconceptions. *Children and Society, 22,* 75–85.

Wolf, J. (2011). *Is breast best? Taking on the breastfeeding experts and the new high stakes of motherhood.* New York: New York University Press.

Zubrick, S., Zubrick, C., Taylor, M., Rice, L., & Slegers, D. (2007). Late language emergence at 24 months: An epidemiological study of prevalence, predictors, and covariates. *Journal of Speech, Language, and Hearing Research, 50,* 1562–1592.

CHAPTER 3

Neuroparenting and the Quest for Natural Authority

Abstract Neuroparenting relies on the authority of nature as providing an eternal, universal, cultureless blueprint for child-rearing but also on the authority of science, as nature's modern interpreter. This chapter critiques the way in which research with animals is used to draw direct inferences for human behaviour in the early years. Bonding and attachment and neuroparenting claims about the neurobiological need for babies to be talked to and played with by their mothers are called into question by anthropological evidence of human variety. Historical examples where spontaneous parental nurture has been construed as a barrier to social progress are discussed and the implications of state action to ameliorate the biological or psychological reproduction of human society are considered.

Keywords Neuroparenting • Nature • Nurture • Authority • Child-rearing • Bonding • Attachment • Enlightenment progress • Biologisation

NATURAL OR SCIENTIFIC PARENTING?

In its most ideological form, the neuroparenting project of improving parenting as a way of improving society appears to problematise modern family practices such as bottle-feeding, putting babies to sleep in their own bedrooms, mothers working and using day care, and the use of

© The Editor(s) (if applicable) and The Author(s) 2016
J. Macvarish, *Neuroparenting*,
DOI 10.1057/978-1-137-54733-0_3

digital media. In wider parenting culture too, these normal (in the UK and USA, majority) ways of caring for children are criticised or worried about as being at odds with 'true' infant needs. The view is often expressed that modern life estranges parents, mothers in particular, from more 'natural' practices of care. The most common way in which this sense of rupture between the natural and the social is expressed is through anxiety about maternal–infant attachment (Riley 1983). When William and Martha Sears coined the term 'attachment parenting' for their recommended style of baby care in 1982, they declared that it could return modern parents to 'common sense' parenting (Sears and Sears 2001). However, this was actually a rejection of what most Western parents thought was common sense at the time.

In the attached parenting style, what is imagined to be 'primitive' infant care is exalted as more attuned to infant needs: prolonged breastfeeding and baby-led weaning; co-sleeping of babies with parents and continuous maternal proximity to the infant through 'baby-wearing' involving the use of slings (Faircloth 2014). The critique of modern methods of baby care, in particular those which attempt to create independent, routinised, self-settling babies, casts them as ignorant, informed by disproven science or outmoded customs, as harmful to children, and productive of adults with embedded psychological problems.

But it is not just modern, Western parenting practices that are problematised by the first three years movement. The US charity Tostan has received a 3.8 million dollar grant from the Hewlett Foundation to bring neuroparenting to poor, rural Senegalese mothers who are said to believe that talking to babies is risky because it might draw out evil spirits (djinns). Three times a week, 'facilitators' in 240 Senegalese villages visit participants' homes for hands-on lessons in how to play constructively with a baby. Tostan chief executive Molly Melching describes how 'We delve into brain development in a non-judgmental way'. She goes on, 'We say, "This is new, even in the United States. We are learning this through new technology."' In the attempt to internationalise the practices of intensive motherhood, metaphors drawn from neuroscience are applied, even in the low-tech environment of rural Senegalese mothers; 'When a mother counts before her baby, the part of the child's brain that deals with maths lights up. We now know the information flows in. If you don't do it, you lose that important time because once your child hasn't got that connectivity part, it will be more difficult to get it later' (Porter 2014). It would be fascinating to know how the local mothers respond to this brain-based parent training. Can a belief in neurons override a belief in djinns? Was the belief in djinns on its way out anyway? Do neurons and djinns develop a relationship with one another?

Echoing the Tostan project in his 2016 Life Chances speech, David Cameron spoke of the need for all parents to learn to perform 'good play' with their children, to ensure their proper brain development. What the Tostan project represents is the globalisation of the first three years movement, but fascinatingly, it seems that whereas in the Anglo-US domain neuroparenting plays to the anti-modern aspects of parenting culture, in the global south, it may be designed to appeal to a modernising aspiration amongst parents. We can see therefore, that babies' brains can simultaneously hold the promise of a return to a better society through the natural and of advancement to a better society through the scientific.

When it comes to talking to and playing with children, the anthropologist David Lancy describes how, '(I)n spite of the lack of strong empirical verification for the direct influence of parent-managed play on child development, a virtual movement has grown up to foster its dissemination' (Lancy 2007, p. 274). This 'parent–child play "cause"', he says, has led to 'attempts to "train" lower-class parents and to export the phenomenon as a fundamental child "right" to the rest of the world' (Lancy 2007, p. 274).

That the overwhelming tone of the critical response to David Cameron's proposal for universal parent training can be characterised as, 'what gives him the authority to tell us how to raise our kids?', should help us to understand the attraction of science and nature to the first three years movement. Whereas the PM's personal knowledge and experience of good parenting was considered open to mockery, the brain, as an embodiment of scientific and natural truth, promises itself as an objective source of family guidance, untainted by the interests and ideologies of society. According to Faircloth (2013), even highly ideological parenting subcultures (such as those committed to attachment parenting), which appear to draw on the past as a guide to infant care as a remedy to the disorientations of modernity, actually rely on the very modern authority of science to ratify that their way is the right way to raise a child. The recourse to nature, and its interpreter, science, as a guide to behaviour reflects a search for a 'cultureless blueprint' for human action and for child-rearing in particular (Faircloth 2015).

Can We Learn from Animals?

The search for this 'cultureless blueprint' often leads towards anthropological studies of simple human societies, of early hominids, or to zoological or psychological studies of animals. Experiments with monkeys, kittens and rats are reported as providing insights for human infant care, often without explicit acknowledgement that the experimental subjects were not human. In 'Our Kids', Robert Putnam draws on a much-cited study of rat behaviour to create a direct analogy between rats licking their young and human mothers acting in a loving way towards their babies:

> Providing physical and emotional security and comfort – hugging, for example – is the human equivalent of a mother rat's licking and grooming behaviour and can make a great difference in children's lives. (Putnam 2015, p. 115)

While animal studies might help us to identify certain fundamental mechanisms by which living things develop, they have severe limitations in their ability to tell us about human emotions or cognition. Rats and monkeys may indeed have their behaviour shaped to a high degree by maternal nurture, and some of their behaviour may look, to a lay observer, like human behaviour. But that does not mean that it is the same behaviour, subject to the same dynamics. Human babies are very different from rats and monkeys even if they seem similarly primitive in their early lives. The biggest difference is that they have an immediately developing consciousness, which brings an open-endedness to their development which is categorically different to that of any animal, even the most sophisticated primates (Guldberg 2010). Besides the obvious problem of comparing conscious humans with unconscious animals, the rat-in-a-lab analogies also rely on a model of human infant care which is atypical of actual human life: a mother, caring for one or more babies in total isolation from other adults. Animal experiments provide neuroparenting advocates with many highly emotive, anthropomorphised vignettes of maternal care which always seem to reinforce the imperative that mothers must care for their babies in a highly attentive, intensive fashion.

In the 1950s and 1960s, US psychologist Harry Harlow's monkey studies became part of popular knowledge about the fundamental need for maternal 'attachment'. Inspired by John Bowlby's WHO-commissioned review, 'Maternal Care and Mental Health' (1952), Harlow experimented on monkeys to prove that in order to thrive, infants need not just physical nurture in the form of food, but emotional nurture in the form of physical contact. The monkeys' need for physical security was interpreted as analogous to the human need to be loved. Films of Harlow's monkeys, tragically clinging to a cold metal mother figure when deprived of the real thing, reached a widespread audience and elicited a strongly empathic, anthropomorphic response in the post-war context of widespread concern about the prevalence of unempathic, disturbed human beings.

Critical Periods and Windows of Opportunity

The over-arching concept which unifies the claims about the need for intensive maternal care is that of 'critical' or 'sensitive' periods in animal and human development. This concept first arose in the 1920s from studies on the effect of toxins on fish embryos. Further studies in embryology in the 1930s found that there were particular points during embryo development when external influences had greater effect. In 1937 Konrad Lorenz studied 'imprinting' in birds, taking the notion of critical periods into postnatal development. Subsequent research experimented with sociability in dogs and emotional development in monkeys.

As more research has been carried out on the concept of critical periods, even in animal studies the fixity of outcome has been disproven for all but a few aspects of development. More characteristic of development is the tendency towards modifiable or reversible outcomes (Bailey et al. 2001, p. 9). Over time, scientists have substituted the term 'sensitive periods' for 'critical periods' to reflect the evidence of more open-ended development, but in neuroparenting, both terms are still used interchangeably, in fact, 'critical' is relied on more often for its connotations of crisis, detached from its origins in a particular scientific hypothesis. In 1979, biologist Patrick Bateson introduced the term 'windows of opportunity' as a more accurate description of animal development than critical or sensitive periods, but in neuroparenting, the term 'windows of opportunity' is used to dramatise an image of a window slamming shut after the critical period of 0–3 or 0–2 ends. It is clear, therefore, that neuroparenting appropriates scientific authority while floating free from scientific rigour or precision.

Bonding and Attachment

Neuroparenting relies on theories of maternal–infant 'bonding' and 'attachment', which claim there is a natural basis to a particularly intensive way of caring for infants. The first three years movement claims that neuroscience has now proved that attachment theory is not only psychologically, but biologically, correct (Kanieski 2010). Yet, according to Gillis (1996), the idea that maternal nurture was a natural thing did not arise until the nineteenth century; before this, it was assumed that caring for infants was a learned practice, not an inherent, feeling-based instinct. Being a woman was not inevitably associated with being a mother, rather, being a wife, skilled at running the household, was viewed as a more important social role. Pregnancy and childbirth were construed as natural processes, but they therefore required certain rituals at their beginning and end by which to mark the separation from, and reintegration into society, of the woman. Motherhood was of more limited significance, symbolically important, but practically, infant care was a task shared by other adults and by older children. Scholars have described how while mothers were responsible for bringing the baby into the world, during the early modern period, socialisation and education were the father's responsibility (Lupton and Barclay 1997; Furedi 2001, 2008).

Historical and anthropological research reveals that human infants have never before been cared for by 'intensive' mothers (Faircloth 2015, pp. 20–21). Are we to conclude that all of the billions of babies who have been carried around by their big sisters, entertained by their older brothers, disciplined by their grandfathers and fed by other mothers grew into neurologically and emotionally dysfunctional adults? The model of the individual mother caring for her individual baby in the home, not simultaneously caring for other children in the family or in the community, nor trying to carry out household labour or paid labour outside the home while the baby is watched by others, is an idealised construction, specific to the present day. It cannot, therefore, be said to be 'natural'.

The extreme, naturalistic attachment parenting model of prolonged breastfeeding, co-sleeping, baby-wearing and elimination communication (where nappies are eschewed) sounds hopelessly unrealistic for most modern families. In order to achieve universal appeal, neuroparenting advice is much more vague about the practical aspects of baby care. However, while the practical side of parenting is not spelled out, the emotional and communicative aspects are extremely prescriptive. This echoes what we heard Sears and Sears say in Chap. 1; the emotional disposition of parents is far more important than 'the rules' of practical care. This explains why the imperative of intensive infant care contained within neuroparenting relies on a belief in the more abstract theory of attachment than on a practical commitment to adopting a totally attached mothering style. Ideas of attachment and bonding in a more nebulous form have considerable power in mainstream contemporary parenting culture. The most concrete way in which this thinking has been institutionalised is in the requirement that staff in maternity wards place newborn babies on their mothers' chests immediately after birth, in order to facilitate 'bonding'. Diane Eyer's detailed analysis of the (unscientific) reasons why this became common practice from the 1970s, concludes that:

> The belief that infants and children are so profoundly shaped by their own mothers that a few hours of contact with them could inoculate them from harm, even enhance their lives for years to come, would seem to border on magical thinking. Yet the idea was readily embraced as a scientific truth because it fit so perfectly with presuppositions about women and infants that have been socially constructed over the course of a century and a half and were threatening to come undone. (Eyer 1992, p. 89)

As Eyer's study shows, the history of the theory of attachment reveals a complex and changing view of the naturalness of mothering. Soon after the Second World War ended, the British psychologist John Bowlby began studying children and adults who demonstrated 'disturbed' (or delinquent) behaviour. He traced this back to their early separation from their mothers. The argument was that babies are naturally desirous of maternal care and mothers are naturally equipped to deliver it. Deprived of this relationship, infants struggle to achieve normal development. Like many child development experts, Bowlby was drawn from his discovery of what he thought was an 'is' in the nature of infant development, to stating some 'oughts' about what society should do. He recommended a number of policies, including marriage guidance to improve the quality of parental relationships and the redistribution of funding from day care services to housekeeping services for mothers, so that they could stay home and concentrate their efforts on child care (Bowlby 1952).

Over time, the conceptualisation of the attachment problem has changed and expanded. Concern about maternal *absence* in the post-World War II period transformed into concern about the quality of maternal *pres-*

ence judged to be insufficiently loving or, indeed, insufficiently 'maternal'. What was the cause of non-maternal mothering? The mothering these inadequate mothers had received from their own mothers. Motherhood thus became pathologised in a 'cycle' model, which could only be broken by therapeutic intervention. Today, all UK mothers have their 'attachment' to their babies assessed by health visitors and the new obsession with pre- and postnatal maternal depression generalises this profoundly pessimistic view of motherhood still further. There is little faith in the 'maternal instinct' today, what is more evident is a negative belief in the difficulty of forming a loving relationship with a baby, and the problems associated with bonding are no longer restricted to mothers; fathers are also encouraged to 'bond' with the foetus in utero by relating to the 'bump', to be present at the birth, maybe cutting the umbilical cord, while they are there, and engaging in 'skin to skin' contact with the newborn. There is more and more talk of paternal depression, both pre- and postnatal. The gender-neutral character of 'parenting' which, to a certain extent, incorporates fathers into the imperative of intensive infant care, therefore contributes to the further denaturalising of the maternal instinct while naturalising the vulnerability of the infant to parental affect.

According to Molly Melching of the Tostan intervention in Senegal, '(P)arenting, for most, isn't nature. It's a learned thing', but Melching's work indicates that this is not learning 'on the job' or from family and community, rather it is training by external experts. For a fundamental characteristic of neuroparenting is that the apparently 'natural' needs of human infants cannot be reliably met by their parents and their communities without special training. And so while the child is natural, the parent is not, rather, the parent is a potentially destructive influence on the child's essential development. And so parenting cannot be adequately performed by recourse to instinct, whether natural or developed through experience and loving feelings, it must be framed by new knowledge from science.

Talking and Playing

Returning to Lancy's fascinating study of mother–infant play, we find further support for the argument that the recent Western norm for infant care, whereby mothers care for young babies largely by themselves, in their own homes, is unusual in historical human terms and therefore the claim that babies 'need' intensive engagement and stimulation to achieve normal brain development, appears to have no biological foundation.

A large survey of anthropological literature cited by Lancy, found that, 'across nearly 200 societies, 40 % of infants and 80 % of toddlers were cared for primarily by someone other than their mother – most commonly, older sisters' (Weisner and Gallimore 1977, cited in Lancy 2007, p. 276).

In most families therefore (and this is surely still true today), siblings are just as much, if not more, of a source of 'stimulation' as parents. Lancy argues that although play is a cultural universal, something which children do spontaneously, and is often continued into adulthood, 'one rarely sees adults playing with children' (Lancy 2007, p. 274). He cites an 'analysis of 186 ethnographies' which showed 'wide variation in the amount of mother-infant play and display of affection' and other research which 'shows that the *en face* position where the mother holds the infant facing her—de rigueur for peek-a-boo—is common in Westernized societies but rare elsewhere, as is the tendency of the mother to talk with the infant' (Lancy 2007, p. 275). In most societies, he proposes, parents are the least likely playmates, because they are usually the ones to impose discipline on the child, and therefore are not necessarily free to be 'playful'. Indeed, it was not until the 1940s that US baby care manuals began to talk of playing with a baby as a maternal duty; before that, play was seen as overstimulating and harmful (Lancy 2007, p. 277).

So we are left with the question once again, did all these other human societies get it wrong? Were their babies under-stimulated and suffering from stunted brain growth? Is it really possible to establish an eternally correct truth of what babies require and is it really likely that we are only now discovering what this might be?

Parents as a Barrier to Progress

We can see that neuroparenting inherently problematises past and present parental care and mobilises expert claims in order to make the case for improving future parenting by specific training, or 'information' and 'support', as it is more often termed. The view that parents pose a barrier to progress can be seen all the way back in Jean-Jacques Rousseau's 'Emile or On Education', published in 1762. For Rousseau, parents are 'the agents who transmit false traditions and habits from one generation to the next' and according to Smeyers, in the mind of Rousseau and the child-centred educators that followed him, 'the adult world, far from representing reason, is essentially corrupt and given over to the superficialities of worldly vanity' (Smeyers 2008, p. 719). This negative view of the adult world and its capacity to socialise its young, tends to view the child as 'essentially good' and 'a product of nature'. The cause of social progress therefore entails making a revolutionary break with existing parental practices; the ideal medium for this, according to Rousseau, was a highly skilled, individual tutor who can allow the child's natural reasonableness to emerge. The parent is sidelined and existing adult wisdom cannot be passed on, social development must be reconstructed in child-led terms.

In contrast, Immanuel Kant (1724–1804) had a more optimistic view of adult society's capacity to socialise its young in enlightened ways, his faith in human reason meant that he could have greater hope for human development. The adult was therefore the moral guide of the child, not vice versa. The Kantian view was that, 'Adulthood shows itself by being in command of oneself, able to bind oneself to a law of one's choosing, to maintain steady relationships both morally and practically and not being reliant upon the judgements of others' (Smeyers 2002, p. 88). The child however, 'is helpless in a moral sense. She does not know what is good and therefore cannot yet take responsibility for her own actions' (Smeyers 2002, p. 88). The parent and later, the teacher, must therefore offer guidance and 'make the necessary decisions in relation to the child' as well as 'confronting the child with rationality' so that the adult may 'awaken the child's potentialities to become a rational human being' (Smeyers 2002, p. 88). Here, parents and other adults have a natural authority, based on their greater experience of moral reasoning and practical judgement.

An interesting practical example of the attempt to change society by improving the nurture of the next generation can be seen in the social experiments of Robert Owen (1771–1858). Owen's 'socialist' community, New Lanark, was based around a cotton mill and its set-up was informed by his belief that humans are infinitely malleable, that moral character was not intrinsic but was the product of the environment in which humans lived. The Owenite equivalents of the 'we now know' and 'the wondrous infant' of neuroparenting are expressed in the metaphors of the fashionable science of his day, chemistry, leading him to describe children as 'without exception, passive and wonderfully contrived compounds' which 'like all the other works of nature, possess endless varieties' of human character, 'yet they partake of that plastic quality, which, by perseverance under judicious management, may be ultimately moulded into the very image of rational wishes and desires' (Owen 1816). Rather than this being a task for the individual parent, moulding the child was a communal project.

According to Owen, the barrier to a fully rational socialisation was the 'partial ignorance of our forefathers' who 'taught their children that which they had themselves been taught, that which they had acquired, and in so doing they acted like their forefathers; who retained the established customs of former generations until better and superior were discovered and made evident to them' (Owen 1816). Although Owen's emphasis on the environmental conditions in which human character is formed and the need to overturn existing parental knowledge seems to have something in common with today's early interventionists, he displayed a rather greater degree of optimism about social change and was ambitious about the human ability to manage and direct it. The difference between Owen and today's early interventionists is that Owen was engaged in a project to transform social relations as a whole. The cultivation of children was not his sole focus; it was part of a greater social experiment in creating the conditions in which humans could be both economically productive and morally autonomous.

The attachment of today's early interventionists to neuroscientised infant determinism reveals their disillusionment with the very possibility of individual moral autonomy or real social change. If people are conceived of as the passive objects of the nurture their brains received in the pre-conscious, early years of life, they can never be said to be truly autonomous; they are the direct products of their parents' traits and dysfunctions. Similarly, the early interventionists refuse to leave parents to exercise their autonomy in the way they raise their children; the first three years project is about normalising the idea that parenting is too difficult for parents to do without recourse to expert training. Significantly, in Owen's communities children under the age of three were raised in the parental home, without interference.

Nature and Nature

If Enlightenment thinkers such as Rousseau, Kant and Owen saw the human essence in man's unique capacity for reason, whatever its source, today's 'thinkers' of the first three years movement see human society as essentially driven by our 'natural' drives. They readily flatten out the distinctions between the human and the natural worlds in order to make their case. In a worldview which sees biologised empathy rather than reason as the basis of the good society, the child is able to lead the way—babies are naturally social and dependent—whereas adults tend to become estranged from one another, losing empathy. For Kant, it is the rational adult that determines society and therefore takes control of the socialisation of children: the role of the parent is to set an example, to be part of the world and to educate the child in moral autonomy and knowledge. In contrast, today's early interventionists have little faith that adults can bear this responsibility. According to them, we must therefore divert the exercise of parental authority through the mediation of expertise which draws not on the authority of reason but on the authority of the natural world, whether in the form of the baby, the brain or science.

By the later nineteenth century, faith in the human capacity for reason and the progressive experiments in social and family living which had followed its celebration in the Enlightenment gave way to a more pessimistic view of humanity. According to Gillis, 'Much of the idealism that had flowed into public life in the first half of the century was redirected to the private sphere thereafter' (1996, p. 100). As the nineteenth century wore on, attention to the protection of children and cultivation of the family became a cultural and political obsession. This conservative turn is exemplified by Herbert Spencer (1820–1903), usually thought of as the strongest exponent of 'laissez-faire', but who, perhaps surprisingly, wrote of the need to school 'the parent of the future' because 'the goodness of a society ultimately depends on the nature of its citizens; and since the nature of its citizens is more modifiable by early training than by anything else, we must conclude that the welfare of the family underlies the welfare of society' (Spencer 1861, p. 10).

Whereas for Robert Owen, social improvement could be brought about by the application of reason to the relationships of production, for Kant by the exercise of total moral responsibility by the individual, and for Rousseau by the cultivation of the child's essential goodness, it is perhaps Spencer who is closest to today's way of thinking:

> As the family comes before the State in order of time as the bringing up of children is possible before the State exists, or when it has ceased to be, whereas the State is rendered possible only by the bringing up of children; it follows that the duties of the parent demand closer attention than those of the citizen. (Spencer 1861, p. 10)

Spencer did not draw on neuroscience or developmental psychology, but on the theory of evolution, which he understood to be an ongoing biological process underpinning human society. According to Burman, as the nineteenth century moved on, political and elite attention turned increasingly to the biological reproduction of society. With very strong echoes of today, '(P)oliticians and the emerging social scientists focused their attention on the "quality" of the population, in particular on those sectors of society considered unstable and unruly' (Burman 2007, p. 18). In 1883, Francis Galton coined the term 'eugenics' to describe the project of managing the 'quality' of human 'stock' through the manipulation of heredity. He also came up with the couplet 'nature and nurture' to connote the innate and the environmental influences on human development, both of which Galton naturalised. The recourse to nature in the extension of evolutionary theory to continued human development married well with the increasing (and justifiable) concern with the living conditions of the poor, and particularly with the welfare of children. What has been called the 'child saving movement' of the late nineteenth century combined reformist concerns for social amelioration with conservative concerns about social disorder. According to the historian Hugh Cunningham, the child came to the fore as a symbol of both anxiety and hope:

> The idea that the child was the key to the future, banal as it sounds, had a definite political message. To say that the child alone held the key to social change was to say that the present generation of adults did not. That, contrary to the hopes of socialists and militant unionists, the social structure could not be transformed within a single generation. Child-centred ideology pictured society inching toward reform generation by generation… Thus the turn-of-the-century exaltation of the child was both romantic and rationalist, conservative and progressive. The child was 'primitive' but this meant it was also malleable, hence really more 'modern' than anyone else. (Cunningham 2006, p. 207)

The Political and Expert Colonisation of Nurture

The turn towards science, nature and the child as a foundation for morality and politics drew first on the natural sciences, but as the nineteenth century turned into the twentieth, it was increasingly associated with psychology. The social project of improving human stock, both in physical and psychological terms, inevitably focused on parents, and on mothers in particular. The cultivation of mothers as a national resource in social improvement was a project evident in the Anglo-American and the European context.

The rise of what has been termed 'scientific motherhood' (Apple 1995, 2006; Ehrenreich and English 1979) on the one hand flattered mothers as being vitally important to national success, but on the other constructed them as in need of expert training. A new layer of experts, in the form of health visitors, home inspectors, social workers and midwives were tasked, first by philanthropic organisations but then directly by the state, with improving maternal skills, in particular by bringing new knowledge about nutrition and hygiene to bear on child care and homemaking.

Many have spotted in neuroparenting, the spectre of eugenics: the return of a concern to correct social structures or secure social order through intervention in the biological. Rather than genetically cleaning up human stock, neuroparenting promises to emotionally engineer a more functional human stock by supporting the 'natural' processes of human emotional development, understood to originate in the nurture of the infant brain. For the twentieth-century philosopher Hannah Arendt, the politicisation of the biological reproduction of humanity is always a dangerous tendency, because it invariably targets and undermines the spontaneous bonds of dependence between humans. The attempt by the state to take over the role of parent has been a feature of all totalitarian regimes and relies on the breaking of the 'spontaneous bonds of dependence' of which Arendt writes. Removing children from their parents is the ultimate exercise of state authority to break these bonds, but the presumption that 'the state knows best' in matters of child-rearing and can therefore engage in projects of parent training also breaks the spontaneous relationship of authority between parents and their children. As Hitler wrote of child-rearing:

> [The] work of care and education must begin with the *young mother*...[I]t must and will be possible, *by a thorough training of...mothers*, to achieve a treatment of the child in his first years that will serve as an excellent basis for future development (Hitler, trans. 1962, in Koonz 1987: 56). (Emphasis added) (Franzblau 1999, p. 27)

At its most extreme, when the individual becomes biologised political property, they are potentially expendable as natural material, not as human beings (as we saw in Nazism and eugenic policies elsewhere).

In the past, the UK proved to be a less fertile ground for the biologised politics of human stock management than was the case in the USA, Sweden and other Nordic states (King 1999). In the UK, the model of the private family headed by morally autonomous parents was forged in part through state action, but within a liberal framework. It has always contained within it the tension between trusting most parents to perform the task of raising the next generation, while policing those parents who fall short of the norms of respectable family life. Up until the late twentieth century, as many have noted, the stick tended to be bent towards trusting the many, while disciplining the few. Successive incarnations of scientific expertise, in the form of medicine, hygiene and psychology, defused and managed the tension between parental authority and state authority, in much the same way that the novelty of neuroscience enters the policy discourse today. But today, the stick is being bent very far in the other direction. As David Cameron declared, the many need parenting classes and the few need their children removed for adoption by better-trained parents:

> it's time to begin talking properly about parenting and babies and reinforcing what a huge choice having a child is in the first place, as well as what a big responsibility parents face in getting these early years right…that must begin by helping those most in need. That's why I've made it such a priority to speed up the adoption process and improve child protection and social services. (Cameron 2016)

We will return to the issue of adoption in Chap. 6.

Tensions Between Determinism and Intervention

Neuroparenting advocates are often self-conscious about the unsavoury past of deterministic thinking and there is sometimes, therefore, an explicit argument in the 0–3 agenda against 'nature' and the fatalism of genetic determinism. Leading neuroparenting advocate Jack Shonkoff argues that they are 'making the case for change', not immutability. When child trauma expert Bruce Perry visited the UK in 2010, he publicly took to task the Conservative MP Iain Duncan Smith for being overly deterministic (and therefore too pessimistic) in his advocacy of early intervention. Perry said that the politician had 'oversimplified' and 'distorted' his findings by implying that neglect or family breakdown could lead to changes in brain size and development (Pemberton 2010). It was a somewhat confusing spat given that Perry's image of the two brains has been a key part of the global dissemination of neuroparenting and he has been described as delivering 'rock-star' style public lectures on the risk to infant brains from bad parenting. In a further twist, the charity Kids Company, which claimed to offer a therapeutic 'fix' to the brains of neglected teenagers, leapt to Duncan Smith's defence while other UK advocates declared their support for Duncan Smith and Perry simultaneously.

This little vignette from the heart of the first three years movement is revealing of the tension between determinism and intervention contained within neuroparenting and reveals that the stronger force in the first three years movement is the interventionist one. This is because the activists and advocates of the movement are not neuroscientised ideologues so much as relatively pragmatic social entrepreneurs who must make the case that their own 'expertise' is crucial in moving society forwards. Their position requires an attachment to the proposition that while there is scope for the exercise of human agency through parenting, it needs to be expert-led (by them). Because the first three years movement is constituted of individuals and bodies with a stake in intervention, they are loathe to concede 'that nothing can be done'.

The Search for Universal Rules of Behaviour

First three years advocates are also very sensitive to the contemporary lack of deference towards claims of political and moral authority. Developmental psychologist and author of the essay 'The Allure of Infant Determinism' (1998), Jerome Kagan, identified one of the appeals of brain-claiming as being their capacity to avoid moralising parental behaviour. They could therefore divert attention from the reality of an absence of consensus about what is right and wrong in family life or the role of the state and offer managerial 'solutions' to social problems through the manipulation of parental behaviour. The problem represented by differential class- or race-based child 'outcomes' is therefore redefined as one of inadequate knowledge and expertise, not right or wrong behaviour. The solution is for parents to commit to improving their knowledge and skills by engaging with expert knowledge to improve the outcomes for the children (Kagan 1998, p. 90).

What is very clear from the anthropological and historical studies discussed in this chapter is that humans raise their young children in ways which reflect the current worldview of that particular society. The values that each society attempts to inculcate in the next generation are those which it currently holds. It is therefore not possible for the child to 'lead the way', since the interpretation of the child will be shaped by that society's views on human agency and the trustworthiness of parental authority. This is not to say that the intergenerational relationship is one-directional or un-dynamic. Each new generation of parents will work with, and work against, the values and ideas of its predecessors, but this is a subtle, creative relationship, enacted within the complex relations of families and between other intimates. At certain historical periods, the improvement of society has been understood as the outcome of political or socially oriented endeavour by engaged adults. At others, it is conceived of in more passive terms, as the outcome of unconsciousness forces such as natural drives or emotions; it is at times such as these that the child tends to be looked to as a guide. But this is dishonest and delusional, the child cannot bear the responsibility of being that guide, and it is rather, used as a Trojan horse inside which various actors, in denial of their interests and in the absence of a coherent ideology, seek to effect social change 'by the back door'. This approach has been called 'socialisation in reverse' (Furedi 2008), that is, parental behaviour is disciplined through their obligation to, and love for, the child rather than vice versa.

Neuroparenting seems to offer a child-centred guide to desirable behaviour that draws on the authority of both an eternalised nature and modern scientific advances. But as we can see, neuroparenting has an ambivalent relationship with nature and a pragmatic, unscientific relationship with science. This is because, rather than being an attempt to engage with scientific discoveries in a wider discussion about moral and political questions, neuroparenting is an attempt to avoid moral and political questions by using science and nature as an eternal, universal, unquestionable source of truth. As we saw in Chap. 2, the neuroscientific confirmation of plasticity, rather than freeing us from a belief in determinism, has coincided with profound anxiety about social bonds and a lack of faith in positive human agency. This has meant that the potentially liberatory open-endedness of human development becomes a source of risk and fear, rather than of resilience and freedom. The plastic brain is rendered 'vulnerable' rather than adaptive, not on the basis of scientific evidence, but because we do not trust parents to raise children well. The argument that the greatest guarantor of social improvement is the project to create babies who are free from negative socialisation, in effect, 'liberated' from untrained, unsupervised parental influence has now been updated and refreshed in the first three years movement, which seeks to bend the stick towards state-monitoring of all parents and away from familial autonomy.

REFERENCES

Apple, R. D. (1995). Constructing mothers: Scientific motherhood in the nineteenth and twentieth centuries. *Social History of Medicine, 8*(2), 161–178.
Apple, R. (2006). *Perfect motherhood: Science and childrearing in America.* New Brunswick/London: Rutgers University Press.
Bailey, D. R., Bruer, J. T., Symons, F. J., & Lichtman, J. W. (2001). *Critical thinking about critical periods.* Baltimore: Paul H. Brookes Publishing.
Bowlby, J. (1995 [1952]). *Maternal care and mental health.* Lanham: Jason Aronson Inc.
Burman, E. (2007). *Deconstructing developmental psychology* (2nd ed.). E.Sussex/New York: Routledge.
Cameron, D. (2016). Prime Minister's speech on life chances. https://www.gov.uk/government/speeches/prime-ministers-speech-on-life-chances. Accessed 5 Feb 2016.
Cunningham, H. (2006). *The invention of childhood.* London: BBC Books.
Ehrenreich, B., & English, D. (1979). *For her own good: 150 years of the experts' advice to women.* London: Pluto Press.
Eyer, D. (1992). *Mother-infant bonding: A scientific fiction.* New Haven/London: Yale University Press.
Faircloth, C. (2013). *Militant lactivism? Infant feeding and maternal accountability in the UK and France.* Oxford/New York: Berghahn Books.
Faircloth, C. (2014). Intensive parenting and the expansion of parenting. In E. Lee, J. Bristow, C. Faircloth, & J. Macvarish (Eds.), *Parenting culture studies.* London: Palgrave MacMillan.
Faircloth, C. (2015). 'Natural' breastfeeding in comparative perspective: feminism, morality, and adaptive accountability. *ETHNOS.* http://www.tandfonline.com/doi/full/10.1080/00141844.2015.1028562
Franzblau, S. (1999). Historicizing attachment theory: Binding the ties that bind. *Feminism and Psychology, 9*(1), 22–31.
Furedi, F. (2001). *Paranoid parenting: Abandon your anxieties and be a good parent.* London: Allen Lane.
Furedi, F. (2008). *Paranoid parenting: Why ignoring the experts may be best for your child* (2nd ed.). London/New York: Continuum.
Gillis, J. R. (1996). *A world of their own making: Myth, ritual, and the quest for family values.* New York: Basic Books.
Guldberg, H. (2010). *Just another ape?* London: Societas.
Kagan, J. (1998). *Three seductive ideas.* Cambridge/London: Harvard University Press.
Kanieski, M. A. (2010). Securing attachment: The shifting medicalization of attachment and attachment disorders. *Health Risk and Society, 12*(4), 335–344.

King, D. (1999). *In the name of liberalism: Illiberal social policy in the USA and Britain*. Oxford/New York: Oxford University Press.

Koonz, C. (1987). *Mothers in the fatherland: Women, the family and Nazi politics*. New York: St Martin's Press.

Lancy, D. F. (2007). Accounting for variability in mother–child play. *American Anthropology, 109*(2), 273–284.

Lorenz, K. (1937). The nature of instinct. In C. Schiller (Ed.), *Instinctive behavior: The development of a modern concept* (pp. 129–175). London: Methuen.

Lupton, D., & Barclay, L. (1997). *Constructing fatherhood: Discourses and experiences*. London: SAGE.

Owen, R. (1816). *A review of society*, second essay. https://www.marxists.org/reference/subject/economics/owen/ch02.htm. Accessed 17 Dec 2015.

Pemberton, C. (2010, April 14). Kids Company rallies to Iain Duncan Smith in brain size row. *Community Care*. http://www.communitycare.co.uk/2010/04/14/kids-company-rallies-to-iain-duncan-smith-in-brain-size-row/

Porter, C. (2014, August 31). Why Senegalese women have been afraid to talk to their babies. *The Star*. http://www.thestar.com/news/world/2014/08/31/why_senegalese_women_have_been_afraid:to_talk_to_their_babies_porter.html. Accessed 10 Jan 2016.

Putnam, R. (2015). *Our kids: The American dream in crisis*. New York: Simon and Schuster.

Riley, D. (1983). *War in the nursery: Theories of the child and mother*. London: Virago.

Sears, W., & Sears, M. (2001). *The attachment parenting book: A commonsense guide to understanding and nurturing your baby*. London: Little, Brown and Company.

Smeyers, P. (2002). The origin: Education, philosophy and the work of art, Chapter 4. In M. A. Peters (Ed.), *Heidegger, education and modernity*. Oxford: Rowman and Littlefield.

Smeyers, P. (2008). Child-rearing: On government intervention and the discourse of experts. *Educational Philosophy and Theory, 40*(6), 719–738.

Spencer, H. (1861). *Education: Intellectual, moral and physical*. London: Manwaring.

CHAPTER 4

Neuroparenting and the State

Abstract The idea that a deficit in British parenting is responsible for many persistent social and economic problems predates the adoption of neuroparenting claims-making by UK policy-makers. The first three years movement mobilises around a set of claims formed in the US policy context but which has been subsequently exported to much of the English-speaking world by 'neuroparenting entrepreneurs', popular disseminators and a process of policy transfer. The rise of the therapeutic state, in which citizens are related to by governments as vulnerable, risky and in need of emotional support, provides the backdrop for the adoption of neuroparenting as a biologised, therapeutic way of conceptualising the relationship between parent and infant.

Keywords Neuroparenting • Parenting • First three years movement • State intervention in the family • Early intervention • Family policy • New Labour • Parenting support • Moral entrepreneurs • Risk • Therapeutic state

It should be clear by now that neuroparenting is a phenomenon emanating less from neuroscience than from operators within the policy domain who together form 'the first three years movement'. Just as the early years determinism that underpins neuroparenting has little to do with science, the first three years 'movement' has little in common with the political and social movements of the twentieth century. It is not a movement with social roots in the populace at large. It does not represent any demand for parenting support made by parents themselves. It is a 'movement' only in the sense that it is a group of people mobilised around a set of ideas, but its dynamic is the product of an interplay between the demand from political actors for legitimising claims and the supply of these claims by a network of advocacy groups, social entrepreneurs, service providers and persuasive individuals. Brain-based claims that 'the first years last for ever' have been honed and disseminated through lobbying, public relations, media work and formal political debates. Their concretisation in copyrighted and commercially marketed programmes of intervention, has allowed them to be rapidly implemented into policy action.

Since the early 2000s, brain-claiming has gained strength in the UK. The list of formal support for the 1001 Critical Days manifesto on its 2015 re-launch demonstrates the range of actors who have adopted the cause of brain-based early intervention. Medical bodies such as the Royal College of Midwives, the Royal College of General Practitioners, the Institute of Health Visiting and the Royal College of Obstetricians and Gynaecologists have signed up. Long-standing children's welfare charities the National Society for the Prevention of Cruelty to Children (NSPCC) and Barnardo's are supporters, as are numerous much smaller non-profits. Also on board are UNICEF, various universities and academic research departments and even Unite, the largest trade union in the UK and Ireland. Psychotherapeutic institutions such as the Bowlby Centre, the Tavistock Centre, the Anna Freud Centre and the Brazelton Centre UK, all have their logos on the most recent manifesto. Also represented are the providers of parenting support programmes CANparent, Mellow Parenting, ParentSkool and Parent Infant Partnership (PiP) UK, many other social enterprises lobbying to have their services bought by government and delivered to parents across the country.

Despite this substantial professional affirmation from across the field of parenting support, when the 1001 Critical Days manifesto was debated in the House of Commons on the last day of business before Christmas in December 2015, there was only a handful of MPs present (I counted 11). All who spoke were strong advocates of the manifesto, some of them quoting directly from it. The low turnout at the parliamentary debate indicates not a lack of interest, but that this is an uncontroversial agenda which does not inspire or require an active democratic mandate to succeed in gaining influence. In fact, most of the manifesto's demands are already in place, if not nationally, then regionally. When David Cameron delivered his Life Chances speech one month after the 1001 Critical Days debate, he did not even refer to that campaign, and yet all of the content could have been lifted directly from it.

A Cause in Search of an Argument

Concern with parental behaviour—with 'nurture'—was a significant feature of the Labour Party's reconstruction as 'New' Labour from the mid-1990s onwards. Discussions about the need for 'parenting support' can be seen in the output of think tanks such as Demos (see Amitai Etzioni's 1995 report, 'The Parenting Deficit') and the Joseph Rowntree Foundation (JRF) (see David Utting's 1995 report 'Family and parenthood: supporting families, preventing breakdown') and within the Labour Party itself (see Straw and Anderson 1996), but it took some years for this to become a totally assumed, uncontested area of political governance. In earlier written material, there is still an acknowledgement that there is an argument to be won in order to legitimise opening up the private world of all families to the purview of the state. Even though the JRF report (1995) contains no references to brains and has to explain what 'parenting' is ('an important mediator between the familiar stresses of adult society and the way that children develop', p. 51), the arguments it puts forward about the significance of the early years, the need for 'parent education', a focus on 'prevention' and the evidence of attachment theory are all familiar today.

This early literature recommends policy initiatives designed to shore up a 'family' perceived to be in crisis and to have lost both its form and its meaning. Our analysis of policy documents found that a consensus had clearly formed from 1997 around the idea of a 'parenting deficit', and the case for 'parenting support' was made in the 1998 green paper, 'Supporting Families' (Home Office 1998). The dominant view was that raising children is both very difficult and of paramount importance, not just to individual families, but to society in general. It was evident that at the turn of the twenty-first century, 'parenting' was in the process of being politicised. And yet references to the brain are not evident in the policy literature until 2003. So, the demand for policy attention to be turned towards the inner workings of the family was established in Britain well before claims entered the scene that 'new evidence from neuroscience' proves that 'the first years last for ever'. In this respect, the 'cause' (intervening in the early years to reshape 'parenting'), can be said to have established itself in policy thinking before the 'argument' (neuroscientific evidence proves that the early years are 'critical').

A significant shift in policy has been identified as occurring in the late 1990s, described by a number of scholars of British social policy as a move from 'implicit' to 'explicit' family policy (Wasoff and Dey 2000; Clarke 2006; Lewis 2011; Henricson 2008). The new approach was characterised by far more direct pronouncements from politicians on how children ought to be raised and an increasing willingness to blame parenting for social ills. One way of understanding the timing of this shift is to recognise that while New Labour moved family life to the centre stage of policy-making from the start of its time in office (1997), the politicisation of family relationships developed through a disavowal of concern for the 'traditional' form of 'the family'. Clear statements were made that there was no going back to a golden age and that this golden age probably never existed. The term 'parenting' entered the policy domain as a way of providing a more gender-neutral, inclusive, less traditionally moralising and stigmatising vocabulary than that of 'family values', 'family breakdown', 'single mothers' or 'feckless fathers' associated with the divisive and discredited Conservative governments of Margaret Thatcher and John Major.

In the UK, the 'parenting support' agenda has been expanded and developed more recently under the umbrella concept of early intervention, but this continues the already-established construction of what Daly calls, 'the most elaborate architecture anywhere for parenting support' (Daly 2013, p. 164). The parenting support agenda has also taken hold in other northern European countries (Martin 2015; Hopman and Knijn 2015) but the UK is seen as leading the way, where new institutions of 'parenting support' and parenting 'expertise' have been established and a growing 'parenting workforce' has been trained (Churchill and Clarke 2009; Gillies 2011). Lewis describes how policy attention has been extended beyond those parents whose children's behaviour has already brought them to the attention of social services, to all parents, who are now encouraged to access universally provided parenting support services in advance of any problems being evident to themselves or others (Lewis 2011). This new approach to family life stands in stark contrast to the UK's 'strong liberal heritage' which held to a norm that the 'family works best when the state and other institutions intervene only in cases of need or crisis' (Daly 2010, p. 433). The early intervention approach was enthusiastically adopted by the Conservative–Liberal Democratic coalition government formed in 2010 and has been pursued by the current majority Conservative administration.

Enter the Neuroscience

It is into this context that neuroscientific claims-making gains traction. The neuroparenting claims which entered the parenting policy frame from 2003 were sourced almost entirely from a discussion which had happened in the USA some years before. In 1994, the US Carnegie Corporation published a report called 'Starting Points: Meeting the Needs of Our Youngest Children', which the historian Elizabeth Hulbert identifies as marking 'the beginnings of a deferral by policy-makers to neuroscience' (2004, p. 311). The report began its discussion of a 'quiet crisis' caused by family change and persistent poverty in dramatic terms; 'Our nation's children under the age of three and their families are in trouble, and their plight worsens every day' (Carnegie Corporation 1994, p. 1). According to Hulbert, although Americans had become 'habituated' to outcries about imperilled children, the attention-grabbing claim of 'Starting Points' was not its doom-laden call to arms but its 'perfectly pitched' claims that a new neuroscientific evidence base existed, proving that the 'quiet crisis' was caused by the child's 'environment' in the earliest years of life (Hulbert 2004, p. 311).

In the same year that 'Starting Points' was published (1994), the Early Head Start programme was launched in the USA, targeting pregnant mothers and their babies up until the age of three. Early intervention arguments increasingly drew on literature which claimed to be finding neurobiological bases for long-standing theories of child development. From 1994, Allan Schore was disseminating his theory of a neurobiological basis for attachment, and in 1997, Rima Shore published 'Rethinking the Brain: New Insights into Early Development', for the Families and Work Institute, Washington. In 2000, Jack Shonkoff and Deborah Phillips published 'From Neurons to Neighbourhoods: The science of early child development', which began to be widely cited in English-speaking policy networks. Shonkoff travelled extensively, promoting the book and disseminating the argument that 'the first years last forever'.

The 'Starting Points' brain-claims were later popularised in the 'I Am Your Child' campaign, launched in 1997 at the White House 'Conference on the Brain', hosted by Bill and Hillary Clinton. This event has been identified as a pivotal moment in the development of the first three years movement (Bruer 1999; Hulbert 2004). 'I Am Your Child' was a slick media campaign, with heavy involvement from Hollywood film director Rob Reiner, which went on to achieve international reach with its celebrity-endorsed and corporate-funded, neuroparenting-advocacy campaign. According to Thompson and Nelson, it 'crystallized the central messages of early brain development for the public' (2001, p. 7). 'I Am Your Child' was subsequently internationalised. Canadian sociologist Glenda Wall describes how the campaign was heavily promoted by the Canadian Institute of Child Health (Wall 2004), while Wilson reports successful lobbying for the campaign in New Zealand (Wilson 2002).

As we noted earlier, it is not until 2003 that brain-claims first enter UK policy, this being evident in the 'Birth to Three Matters' literature review, but the terrain of parenting support was by then established, most evidently in the Sure Start initiative, launched in 1998. Neuroscientific claims-making about child outcomes strengthened the argument that family life was a legitimate target of policy and promised to establish objective measures of parental improvement for policy evaluation. Labour Children's Minister Margaret Hodge put forward the new way of thinking in explicit terms:

> Driven as we are by a belief in equality of opportunity and fairness of outcome, the knowledge that the early years of a child's life are crucial in determining the outcomes for children when they grow up, means we must focus our energy and resources on the early years. For the Right the agenda is different. They believe that the early years remain the private concern of families, with the state only intervening when things go wrong. (Hodge 2004, Speech to the Social Market Foundation, 1 May)

In 2005, New Labour hardened up its parenting support mission with the 'Respect Agenda', focusing on 'anti-social' families and notoriously becoming associated with the idea of 'baby ASBOs' (anti-social behaviour orders), when PM Tony Blair claimed that through the identification of risk factors, it was now possible to predict, while still *in utero*, which babies would become future criminals. This proposition was ridiculed more because of its punitive-sounding 'law and order' character than its extraordinary predictive claim. A year later, the then leader of the Conservative opposition, David Cameron, was equally mocked for his so-called 'Hug a Hoodie' speech, in which, influenced by neuroadvocate Camila Bathmanghelidjh of Kids Company, he sought to rebrand the Conservative Party as in-touch and caring, by talking about the emotional causes of teenage delinquency.

Val Gillies suggests that it was the lack of evidence of success for existing parenting interventions such as Sure Start, which led policy-makers to adopt brain-claims from America. She also argues that brain-based early intervention 'offered a particularly useful narrative in the context of the austerity drive' in response to the 2008 recession, providing 'an evidenced, boundaried and very cost limited policy approach' (Gillies 2011 see also Edwards et al. 2015a, b). Things certainly speeded up from 2008, when three reports emerged in quick succession making the case for early intervention using the strongest brain terms yet. In the first report, it was claimed that:

> Neuroscience can now explain why early conditions are so crucial: effectively, our brains are largely formed by what we experience in early life…scientific discoveries suggest it is nurture rather than nature that plays the lead role in creating the human personality … It has been said that 'the greatest gift for a baby is maternal responsiveness'. The more positive stimuli a baby is given, the more brain cells and synapses it will be able to develop. (Allen and Duncan Smith 2008, p. 57)

Two subsequent reports, commissioned by the government, were similarly brain-centred, with Bruce Perry's image of the normal and the 'shrivelled' brain featuring prominently on the front covers (Allen 2011a, b). This was a period when neuroparenting arguments for early intervention were vigorously lobbied for in the central policy domain. In other areas of government, neuroparenting was also establishing itself. Brain-claims are evident in maternal and infant health policy (DH 2008), child protection (Munro 2011; Narey 2009), public health (Marmot 2010) and early years education (Tickell 2011a). Typically, the same claims were repeated, often with no references given to the source. In this maternal health document setting out the 'Child Health Promotion Programme: Pregnancy and the First Five Years of Life', without referring to any evidence, it is argued that policy needs to

> reflect new evidence that has emerged about neurological development and the importance of forming a strong child-parent attachment in the first years of life. It should also incorporate the information that we have about the adverse effect that maternal anxiety and depression in pregnancy can have on child development. A child's brain develops rapidly in the first two years of life, and is influenced by the emotional and physical environment as well as by genetic factors. Early interactions directly affect the way the brain is wired, and early relationships set the 'thermostat' for later control of the

stress response. This all underlines the significance of pregnancy and the first years of life, and the need for mothers and fathers to be supported during this time. (DH 2008, p. 9)

Recent research on the appeal of brain-claiming to policy actors suggests that the visual presentations of the impact of neglect and abuse on infant brains have a strong impact when making the case for funding (Broer and Pickersgill 2015; Bowen et al. 2009; Lawless et al. 2013). At a time when public sector spending has been dramatically squeezed, each sector of early years services could make the case for its own preservation by emphasising the vital importance of its work for infant brain development. As one policy advisor in the early years put it in a study of the experience of brain-claiming amongst public sector officials:

> if you tell a society that the way in which they nurture children changes the way their brain develops, and you show them pictures that corroborate that, it's pretty compelling. No one wants to damage a child's brain, or to deny a child the opportunity to develop their brain properly. It's emotive, and it's powerful. (Broer and Pickersgill 2015, p. 55)

NEUROPARENTING ENTREPRENEURS

There is a relatively small number of key players who have shaped the neurobiological claims-making of the first three years movement in the UK; we will not discuss them all here but pick the most prominent to give an idea of the roles they have played in formulating and disseminating the neuroparenting argument. Adapting Howard Becker's concept 'moral entrepreneurs' as a description of advocates who drive the construction of particular moral or social problems, we might call these individuals, 'neuroparenting entrepreneurs' (Becker 1963). The most significant is Professor Jack Shonkoff, paediatrician, co-author of the globally influential report 'From Neurons to Neighbourhoods: The Science of Early Child Development' and Director of the Harvard Center on the Developing Child. According to Becker, 'moral entrepreneurs' define an issue by the language and concepts they choose, they frame and typify social problems by defining the framework of knowledge by which it should be understood. As we discussed in the previous chapter, this is certainly an apt description of Jack Shonkoff's work to create 'translational' metaphors of brain development that can operate in the policy domain and in public discourse.

Another very important voice in neuroparenting advocacy is Bruce D. Perry. Perry is an American psychiatrist whose populist books, 'The Boy Who Was Raised as a Dog' (2006) and 'Born For Love: why empathy is essential—and endangered' (2010) have achieved high levels of publicity in the USA. Perry rose to media prominence after serving as an expert witness in the inquiry into the 1999 Columbine school massacre, but he claims previously to have been involved in the aftermath of the Waco siege in 1993 and the Oklahoma City bombing in 1995 and in high-profile work on Post-Traumatic Stress Disorder (PTSD) and allegations of ritual abuse. In 2005, Perry toured New Zealand, in 2012, Australia, and in 2010 and 2014 he came to the UK. According to a newspaper report of this latest UK visit, Perry met 'senior government ministers' including 'the prisons minister...and the health secretary', he also 'spoke with Labour's shadow education and treasury teams, and the cabinet secretary, Sir Jeremy Heywood' (Butler 2014). Despite Perry's protestations, discussed in the previous chapter, that his brain-claims were being exaggerated by policy-makers, the journalist describes how the psychiatrist's 'vivid style is to stitch together data, shocking anecdotes and emotive imagery, such as a video clip of a young Ukrainian woman, Oxana Malaya, who wanders around on all fours: a legacy, it seems, of her early years when she was neglected by her parents and spent five years, apparently, in the company of a pack of dogs'. Perry reportedly says that 'the neuroscience simply helps persuade reluctant policymakers', making 'people who are uncomfortable with social sciences think that somehow it [the benefit of early intervention] is real' (Butler 2014). Similar reports emerge from Perry's visit to Australia. The *Sydney Morning Herald* describes, how 'Perry's unusual hour-long meeting with Cabinet followed his day-long presentation to a mostly adoring audience of 900'. This was apparently 'one of the biggest turn-outs in years for a fee-paying seminar on children, and Perry's rock star-like performance, as well as his slides showing the shrunken brains of neglected children, had the sort of impact to swell the ranks' (*Sydney Morning Herald*, 13 May 2000 cited in Bowen et al. 2009).

George Hosking of The Wave Trust (Worldwide Alternatives to Violence), has also been influential in UK neuroparenting. The trust was set up in 1996 and their influence in formulating neuroparenting claims and disseminating them through publications, public events and private lobbying has been considerable. Hosking co-wrote the 2008 and 2009 reports 'Early Intervention: Good Parents, Great Kids, Better Citizens' and both of Graham Allen's subsequent reports. Bruce Perry is listed as a research adviser to the trust, and according to the trust's website, they are funded by 'national and local government bodies, police forces, foundations and trusts, as well as donations from private individuals' (Wave Trust 2016).

British politicians who have played a key role in advocating neuroparenting in parliament, to the media, amongst the third sector and in local and regional government are Graham Allen, Andrea Leadsom and more recently, Tim Loughton, all of whom are active in 1001 Critical Days. Leadsom in particular, speaks dramatically about the effect of bad parenting on babies' brains and has publicly shared her own experience of post-natal depression:

> 'If you're left to scream and scream day after day, your levels of cortisol remain high and you develop a slight immunity to your own stress, so what you find is babies who have been neglected tend to become risk-takers,' Leadsom says. 'The worst thing, however, is the parent who is inconsistent – you know: sometimes when I cry my mum hugs me and other times she hits me. That is where the baby develops an antisocial tendency. Kids who go and stab their best mate, or men who go out with a woman and rape and strangle her – these are the kinds of people who would have had very distorted early experiences.' (Rustin 2012)

Leadsom has also served as a trustee on Oxford Parent Infant Project (OXPiP), one of the parenting intervention programmes currently being rolled out nationally.

The American economist James Heckman has also become increasingly prominent in the first three years advocacy. His work combines mathematical modelling, child development and brain science to make the case for early intervention. According to professor of social work Sue White, this is 'very attractive to policy-makers as it promises a rigorous scientific basis to guide public investment', not only that, as it is 'focused on children, it appeals to both left and right, as the entitlements of the very young are not sullied by any moral stain their parents may carry' (White and Wastell 2015, p. 4).

Popular Disseminators

We have given little attention so far to the promotion of neuroparenting in the broader public discourse of the media or to commercially produced parenting advice material. There are few a notable neuroparenting entrepreneurs who operate outside the policy domain, but whose influence often crosses over into the policy discourse. In the UK, these are most famously, Penelope Leach (mentioned in Chap. 2 for her comments on the 'toxic stress' experienced by crying babies), Sue Gerhardt, author of 'Why Love Matters: How affection shapes a baby's brain' (2004), Aric Sigman, a regular media commentator and Margot Sunderland, author of 'What Every Parent Needs to Know: The incredible effects of love, nurture and play on your child's development' (2006, 2007). Leach, Gerhardt and Sunderland have both popular and professional influence, with their books cited in maternal health literature and used in the training of midwives and health visitors.

Studies of media coverage of neuroparenting show there is a strong appetite among publishers for brain-claiming which dramatises both the threats to the brain and the opportunities for optimising brain capacity with the right kind of parental nurture (O'Connor and Joffe 2012). Here, *Guardian* columnist Polly Toynbee demonstrates the way in which brain-talk can dramatise the advocacy of early intervention:

> Research has for decades kept proving that, by the age of three, a child's destiny is all but sealed by how much affection, conversation, reading and explaining they have received. Getting no love and no language relegates them to a lesser life. Recent research from the University of Pennsylvania scanned children's brains over 20 years and found cognitive stimulation by the age of four was the key factor in developing the cortex, predicting cognitive ability 15 years later. That shows how brief is the window of opportunity for changing lives. (Toynbee 2012)

What the above sketch of the development of neuroparenting and the early intervention agenda in the UK indicates is that: one, it floats above any party politics and allows new political alliances to form; two, it relies heavily on arguments, evidence and entrepreneurs from the USA and three, there is a very close relationship between policy advocates, politicians and the third sector.

The Therapeutic State

To further understand the significance of the turn to early intervention, we will now consider it in relation to the concepts of 'therapy culture' and the 'therapeutic state' (Furedi 2004; Nolan 1998). These authors conceptualise what has become a framework for negotiating the relationship between the individual and society or the state, which sees the individual as relatively weak or vulnerable and therefore in need of therapeutic support. Furedi traces this development in the UK to the 1970s but describes it as gaining strength in the 1980s when there was 'a shift of focus from problems rooted in the social realm to emotional turmoil':

> During the economic upheavals of the early 1980s, even radical critics of society began to emphasise the mental health consequences of free-market capitalism. As they grappled with the a growing mood of disenchantment with trade union militancy and redistributionist politics, many activists became drawn towards protesting about the mental health consequences of inequalities. (Furedi 2004, p. 27)

Furedi also sees in this development a therapeutic reinvention of the old 'cycles of degeneracy' or 'cycles of poverty' arguments which had been rejected by the UK elite in the 1960s, even while they gained purchase in the USA (Welshman 2008). In this framework of environmental diagnoses of causation, problematic emotions are not just the consequences of problems such as poverty, racism, poor parenting and domestic violence, but the cause of these problems. Over recent years, the 'environment' has been narrowed from the economy and society, to the community, to the family and now to the individual parent, constructing an outlook of 'emotional determinism' in which 'unprocessed and unmanaged emotions are the cause of the ills that afflict society'; ultimately, Furedi explains, '(T)he belief that 'it all goes back to the womb' is the axial principle of emotional determinism' (Furedi 2004, p. 29).

US sociologists Berger and Berger, back in the 1980s, described the rise of a 'knowledge class' in the USA, which is dependent on state funding and is key to the development of claims about the nature of the individual, about the relationship between the public and private sphere and which seeks to re-orient politics around a concern for the cultivation of vulnerable individuals (Berger and Berger 1983). This description seems to fit with the new professionals of the parenting support workforce and the advocates of neuroparenting more generally. It is difficult not to think that for all the talk of the need for 'secure attachments' between parents and children, the real attachment anxiety emanates from the early years professionals understandably fearful of public spending cuts, and the funding-hungry third sector organisations, keen to get their services commissioned by government.

The politicisation of concern for the relationship between intimate relations and social order was first evident in the USA. The social disruption of the 1930s was responded to with the New Deal, which incorporated something of a turn towards the emotions, with an emphasis on 'New Deal, New Self' and increased political talk of 'feelings'. In the 1940s and 1950s, the influence of paediatric psychiatrist John Bowlby was indicative of a similar way of thinking in Europe. In 1949, the WHO-commissioned Bowlby to review research on the mental health of homeless children in post-war Europe, resulting in his 'Maternal Care and Mental Health' report, published in 1951. His main conclusions, that 'the infant and young child should experience a warm, intimate, and continuous relationship with his mother (or permanent mother substitute) in which both find satisfaction and enjoyment' influenced practices of care for children in hospitals and other institutions but were also disputed both conceptually and evidentially. Even so, 'attachment' became a potent metaphor for the disruptions to social bonds and family relationships caused by the Second World War: evacuation policies, huge numbers of refugees, women serving the war effort in the workplace and the establishing of state nurseries. The concern here was not with a residuum—there was full employment, so no 'underclass'—but a more nebulous sense of unease about social and moral disorientation.

In the 1950s, concern about juvenile delinquency was rife, but it was not until the 1960s that poverty became located as the problem, when, in the USA, the antecedents of early intervention were laid in Lyndon Johnson's 'War on Poverty', a political programme which led to pre-school initiatives such as Head Start. Launched in 1964, Head Start was initially a summer enrichment programme for underprivileged children immediately prior to starting school. It sought to help children achieve their full potential by improving not just their pre-school educational experience but by improving the 'feeling home'. A concern with youth delinquency in particular, was associated with these initiatives. Subsequent programmes such as the HighScope Perry Preschool Project (1962–7), the Abecedarian Program (1972–85) and the Nurse Family Partnership (early 1970s) focused on the home and maternal care in particular. These three programmes are still drawn upon by advocates of early intervention today, despite poor evidence that they achieved any lasting impact. The response of the first three years movement to these ambiguously successful programmes has been to advocate even earlier intervention and to argue for this using neuroscience.

Are We All Dysfunctional Now?

There are many continuities apparent in the resurrection of nineteenth-century concerns about social disorder and dysfunctional people: worklessness, intoxication, brutalised and violent interpersonal relationships, financial and parental irresponsibility have long been identified as problems to be managed. But a striking feature of today's neuroparenting thinking is the expansion from 'problem groups' who are distinguished by the lack of adherence to social norms, to a universal claim that parenting is generally so important and so difficult that it cannot be left to parents. So the message today is a more universal, less moralistic one than in the nineteenth century: all parents struggle, it's not to do with failure on our part but the inherent difficulty of the task.

References

Allen, G. (2011a). *Early intervention: The next steps.* London: Cabinet Office.
Allen, G. (2011b). *Early intervention: Smart investment, massive savings.* London: Cabinet Office.
Allen, G., & Duncan Smith, I. (2008). *Early intervention: Good parents, great kids, better citizens.* London: Centre for Social Justice and the Smith Institute.
Becker, H. (1963). Moral entrepreneurs. In *Outsiders* (pp. 147–163). New York: The Free Press.
Berger, B., & Berger, P. (1983). *The war over the family: Capturing the middle ground.* New York: Anchor Press/Doubleday.
Bowen, S., Zwi, A., Sainsbury, P., & Whitehead, M. (2009). Killer facts, politics and other influences: What evidence triggered early childhood intervention policies in Australia? *Evidence & Policy, 5*(1), 5–32.
Broer, T., & Pickersgill, M. (2015). Low expectations, legitimization, and the contingent uses of scientific knowledge: Engagements with neuroscience in Scottish social policy and services. *Engaging Science, Technology, and Society, 1*, 47–66.
Bruer, J. (1999). *The myth of the first three years: A new understanding of early brain development and lifelong learning.* New York: The Free Press.
Butler, P. (2014, May 6). Policymakers seduced by neuroscience to justify early intervention agenda. *The Guardian.*
Churchill, H., & Clarke, K. (2009). Investing in parenting education: A critical review of policy and provision in England. *Social Policy and Society, 9*(1), 39–53.
Clarke, K. (2006). Childhood, parenting and early intervention: A critical examination of the Sure Start national programme. *Critical Social Policy, 26*(4), 699–721.
Corporation, C. (1994). *Starting points: Meeting the needs of our youngest children, abridged version.* New York: Carnegie Corporation.

Daly, M. (2010). Shifts in family policy in the UK under New Labour. *Journal of European Social Policy, 20*(5), 433–443.

Daly, M. (2013). Parenting support policies in Europe. *Families Relationships and Societies, 2*(2), 159–174.

Department of Health (DH). (2008). *The Child Health Promotion Programme: Pregnancy and the first five years of life*. London: DH.

Edwards, R., Gillies, V., & Horsley, N. (2015a). Brain science and early years policy: Hopeful ethos or 'cruel optimism'? *Critical Social Policy, 35*(2), 167–187.

Edwards, R., Gillies, V., & Horsley, N. (2015b). Early intervention and evidence-based policy and practice: Framing and taming. *Social Policy and Society, 15*, 1–14.

Etzioni, A. (1995). *The parenting deficit*. London: Demos.

Furedi, F. (2004). *Therapy culture: Cultivating vulnerability in an uncertain age*. London: Routledge.

Gerhardt, S. (2004). *Why love matters: How affection shapes a baby's brain*. London: Routledge.

Gillies, V. (2011). From function to competence: Engaging with the new politics of family. *Sociological Research Online, 16*(4), 11. http://www.socresonline.org.uk/16/4/11.html

Henricson, C. (2008). Governing parenting: Is there a case for a policy review and statement of parenting rights and responsibilities? *Journal of Law and Society, 35*(1), 150–165.

Hodge, M. (2004). Speech to the Social Market Foundation, 1st May, cited in Gillies (2013) see above.

Home Office. (1998). *Supporting families: A consultation document*. London: Home Office.

Hopman, M., & Knijn, T. (2015). The 'turn to parenting': Paradigm shift or work in progress? *International Journal of Child Care and Education Policy, 9*, 10.

Hulbert, A. (2004). *Raising America, experts, parents, and a century of advice about children*. New York: Vintage.

Lawless, A., Coveney, J., & MacDougall, C. (2013). Infant mental health promotion and the discourse of risk. *Sociology of Health and Illness, 36*(3), 416–431.

Lewis, J. (2011). Parenting programmes in England: Policy development and implementation issues, 2005–2010. *Journal of Social Welfare and Family Law, 33*(2), 107–21.

Marmot, M. G., Allen, J., Goldblatt, P., Boyce, T., McNeish, D., Grady, M., & Geddes, I. (2010). *Fair society, healthy lives: The Marmot Review: Strategic review of health inequalities in England post-2010*. London: Department of Health.

Martin, C. (2015). Parenting support in France: Policy in an ideological battlefield. *Social Policy and Society*, First View Article, July 1–12.

Munro, E. (2011). *The Munro review of child protection: Final report, a child-centred system* (Vol. 8062). London: The Stationery Office.

Narey, M. (2009). *Report from the Independent Commission on Social Mobility.* London: Liberal Democrats.

Nolan, J. (1998). *The therapeutic state: Justifying government at century's end.* New York: New York University Press.

O'Connor, C., & Joffe, H. (2012). Media representations of early human development: Protecting, feeding and loving the developing brain. *Social Science and Medicine, 97,* 297–306.

Perry, B., & Szalavitz, M. (2006). *The boy who was raised as a dog and other stories from a child psychiatrist's notebook.* New York: Basic Books.

Perry, B., & Szalavitz, M. (2010). *Born for Love: Why empathy is essential—And endangered.* New York: Harper Collins.

Phillips, D. A., & Shonkoff, J. P. (Eds.). (2000). *From neurons to neighborhoods: The science of early childhood development.* Washington, DC: National Academies Press.

Rustin, S. (2012, November, 27). Andrea Leadsom: Lobbying for more support for parents and children. *The Guardian.* http://www.theguardian.com/society/2012/nov/27/andrea-leadsom-lobbying-parents-children. Accessed 17 Jan 2016.

Straw, J., & Anderson, J. (1996). *Parenting: A discussion paper.* London: The Labour Party.

Sunderland, M. (2006/2007) *What every parent needs to know: The remarkable effects of love, nurture and play on your child's development.* London: Dorling and Kindersley.

Thompson, R. A., & Nelson, C. A. (2001). Developmental science and the media: Early brain development. *American Psychologist, 56*(1), 5–15.

Tickell, D. C. (2011a). *The early years: Foundations for life, health and learning : An independent report on the Early Years Foundation Stage to Her Majesty's Government.* London: Department of Education.

Toynbee, P. (2012, October 18). Of all the wild Tory dogma, this cut-price baby farming is the worst. *The Guardian.* http://www.theguardian.com/commentisfree/2012/oct/18/tory-dogma-cut-price-baby-farming. Accessed 17 Jan 2016.

Utting, D. (1995). *Family and parenthood: Supporting families, preventing breakdown.* York: Joseph Rowntree Foundation.

Wall, G. (2004). Is your child's brain potential maximized?: Mothering in an age of new brain research. *Atlantis, 28*(2), 41–50.

Wasoff, F., & Dey, I. (2000). *Family policy.* Oxon: Routledge.

Wave Trust. (2016). http://www.wavetrust.org/. Accessed 12 Feb 2016.

Welshman, J. (2008). The cycle of deprivation: Myths and misconceptions. *Children and Society, 22,* 75–85.

White, S., & Wastell, D. (2015). The rise and rise of prevention science in UK family welfare: Surveillance gets under the skin. *Families, Relationships and Societies.* http://dx.doi.org/10.1332/204674315X14479283041843.

Wilson, H. (2002). Brain science, early intervention and "at risk" families: Implications for parents, professionals and social policy. *Social Policy and Society, 1*(3), 191–202.

CHAPTER 5

Getting Inside the Family

Abstract Neuroparenting promises to make the quality and quantity of parental love measurable and improvable. Love and care within the family become instrumentalised in the project of creating better citizens. Parental authority is substituted for the authority of the expert, the parental role is professionalised and is idealised as a 'cooled', arms-length process of behaviour management. While parents are prioritised as the primary determinate of their child's future, the importance of this role means that they are encouraged to see help-seeking (from official sources) as the most important rule of parenting. The intimate practices, rituals and pleasures of family life are potentially undermined by the neuroparenting promotion of new rituals, or the instrumentalised reinterpretation of old ones.

Keywords Neuroparenting • Intimacy • Parental nurture • Instrumentalisation • Regulation of intimacy • Cultural cooling • Parenting support • Family rituals

We discussed in Chap. 2 how early years advocates in the USA set out to challenge 'the family bubble', by which they meant the presumption that parents must bear most of the responsibility for raising young children. The aim of persuading society that it must share the burden of raising the next generation is a commendable one which in other eras would

© The Editor(s) (if applicable) and The Author(s) 2016
J. Macvarish, *Neuroparenting*,
DOI 10.1057/978-1-137-54733-0_5

have been translated into public funding for kindergartens, high-quality public schooling, leisure and cultural facilities, good infrastructure and workers' rights. However, those making the demand today for greater social responsibility for raising children through the first three years movement demand none of these things. Instead they focus their attention less on social provision in support of the child than on state intervention to improve the parent.

The project of improving the parent leads to actions aimed at altering emotional dispositions and regulating the minutiae of moment-by-moment parent–child interactions. As a recent study of influential individuals working in the field of parenting support found, the preoccupation of policy therefore becomes getting 'into the home' (Daly and Bray 2015, p. 637). In this chapter, we will explore how the drive for better parenting pushes the state deeper and deeper into the home, and into the most intimate relationships of the family.

Winning the argument for parenting support has not been a straightforward process; it has been reworked over the years, with different organisations and individuals coming to the fore at different times. Changes of government have led to different players and varying emphases dominating, but there has been a continuous movement in the same direction: towards the opening up of what goes on behind the closed doors of the family to external guidance. We have now reached a point where critical voices are barely heard and the new class of parent trainers simply assume their project is uncontroversial. From the study cited above, it seems so; the interviewees thought it appropriate and necessary to help parents 'with the everyday challenges of raising children'; this rarely required explanation or justification and there was 'little internal questioning about the general endeavour of parenting support' within their field (Daly and Bray 2015, p. 638).

In the previous chapter, we discussed the development since the 1990s of a 'therapeutic' state. By this we do not mean a soft, touchy-feely state, but one which creates a more intimate and direct relationship with the population as individuals. In the same way that parents are encouraged to directly attune themselves to what might be going on inside the heads of their babies in order to better manage their emotions and behaviour, so new ways of operating have become part of state action which, with less and less apology, treats more and more citizens as prone to dysfunction and in need of expert management.

The study of neuroparenting provides a case study of how this occurs in one particularly significant area of public discourse and policy action. In the final chapter, we will draw out the dangers of this development and make the case for resistance to it, but here we will describe how the case has been made for turning state attention towards the home and the parental mind.

Instrumentalising Everyday Life

Neuroparenting targets the everyday challenges of raising children and the most intimate aspects of baby care, but for all the talk of scanners, synapses and neurons, neuroparenting advice is remarkably prosaic. The Canadian '7 Ways to Build Your Baby's Brain Power' leaflets encourage parents to 'Touch, Talk, Read, Smile, Sing, Count, Play'. The UK's Five to Thrive campaign gives parents five simple daily targets: 'Talk, Play, Relax, Cuddle, Respond'. Presumably all parents, to a greater or lesser degree, 'talk, cuddle, smile, sing, play, read, count and relax' with their children, so what exactly are these parenting experts trying to get us to do differently? There are three things:

1. To 'parent' our children, not just be 'parents'. This means actively, consciously considering our everyday actions as significant for the child's long-term development.
2. To do more of the talking, smiling, singing, counting, playing, cuddling, relaxing, reading. In some instances, experts try to quantify a recommended daily 'dose' of these activities, but generally, the advice is just to 'do more'.
3. To accept the need for advice and support from professional parent support workers.

In neuroparenting, the claim that all parents need to be told in what way they should relate to their children, and how often they should perform certain prescribed interactions is justified by the brain-building significance attached to parent–child interactions, but relies on a presumption of parental ignorance or inertia. A report from the National Literacy Trust's 'Talk to Your Baby' campaign provides a more subtle example of this. Despite acknowledging that most parents 'do not really need to be told how or why they should interact with their baby' and suggesting that it is 'instinctive for most parents to start the moment their baby is born', the authors immediately raise the spectre of 'one in 10 mothers' having 'some level of post-natal depression, which may affect interaction' and soon contradict their initial faith in parental instinct by asserting that 'early communication is so important that all parents can be reminded from time to time to talk, listen and respond to their child' in order to 'enrich the experience for both parent and child'. Apparently, parents 'may not always recognise how much their child relies on them to learn to talk and communicate effectively' (National Literacy Trust 2005, p. 5). The report as a whole treads a careful line between avoiding an overly negative view of the state of British parenting while still making the case for its own campaign to train parents in instilling 'pre-literacy' skills in their infants to remedy a 'fall' in the communication skills of young children which they admit is not proven but 'perceived'.

The idea of a communication deficit is also evident in a report from the All Party Parliamentary Sure Start Group (2013), which says 'too many parents do not know the importance' of talking, singing and playing for their children's life chances. Children's Centres, therefore, 'have a key role to play in changing this, both through the direct provision of activities which in particular support emotional resilience, communication and language development' but also through 'giving parents the information, confidence and support they need to create a stimulating home learning environment for their babies and children' (AAPSSG 2013).

The idea that parents do not appreciate their own significance and by implication are unable to accept full responsibility for raising their child runs throughout the expert claims. Bolstering parental 'confidence' is therefore required so that they can perform the necessary tasks of parent–child interaction, consciously enough and frequently enough. But it seems highly unlikely that parents could fail to understand themselves to be the most important people in their children's lives as this responsibility is experienced moment by moment in parenthood. It also seems unlikely that parents conceive of the way they relate to their children as a series of 'tasks' and 'interactions' which could be separated out, labelled and measured.

When we gaze into our baby's eyes while feeding them because we find them the most beautiful and wondrous baby in the world, we are doing something different from gazing into their eyes because we have read in a baby manual or been told by our midwife that this is good 'bonding' practice. When we absent-mindedly nuzzle our newborn's head because they smell delicious, or stroke their feet because they are unbelievably perfect and tiny, we are touching for entirely different reasons than those we are taught are important in a neuro-stimulating baby massage class. Talking to our newborns about all kinds of nonsense when we are going a bit crazy from being at home with them on a wet weekend is not the same as talking to our babies because we have been told by the PM that it is neurologically critical and will increase their grades at school. These are the kinds of moments that make having babies pleasurable, rewarding and fun, but what is the difference between doing them spontaneously and doing them because we have been told that they matter?

Absent-mindedly nuzzling a baby's head is a sensual, spontaneous act that pleases the nuzzler but would be discontinued if it unsettled the infant, it is intrinsically responsive. Talking to babies can be amusing to us because they don't understand what we are saying but are nevertheless interested in, or soothed by our voices. Contrast this to the official advice given to Sure Start centre staff:

1. During 'stay and play' and other appropriate sessions, Centre staff should support and facilitate parents to play with their babies and children in ways that encourage their development – emphasising the benefits of talking to children and affectionate praise.
2. Centres should either provide or promote local singing and story sessions which encourage parents to sing with their babies and children and promote the benefits of reading even to very young children (All Party Parliamentary Sure Start Group 2013).

We can see that parent training instrumentalises the everyday acts of love and care that parents spontaneously carry out, not because they want to build their baby's brain, but because they find them intrinsically rewarding. When we do these things, we have a perspective that is internal to the relationship between us and our child, and we enjoy the feeling of being unself-conscious. The funny thing about babies and young children is that their lack of self-consciousness seems to be infectious, demanding of us an immediate, spontaneous response that is playful and loving. Some adults spontaneously enjoy this, others do not and feel uncomfortable, but most parents will let down their guard with their own children in private, even if they struggle to do it with other people's children or in front of other adults. What is important here is privacy, for few of us are unself-conscious in the presence of any but a very small number of trusted, intimate companions. Yet the parent trainers want us to feel able (or compelled?) to 'perform' this intimate talking and playing, any place, any time:

> 3. Ante- and post-natal groups in Centres should encourage parents to speak to their baby, particularly in affectionate tones, despite the fact that they are not yet able to reply. They should help parents overcome any sense of shyness or embarrassment about doing so, particularly in public. (All Party Parliamentary Sure Start Group 2013)

Within the family, our private selves are at play. The trust, rituals and shared meanings which exist in our intimate family lives are vital to our ability to exist in the world in the roundest sense (Bristow 2016). But for family relationships to be truly intimate, and to be uniquely life-sustaining as such, we need to feel that the meanings through which we act there are specific to 'us', as individual members of a particular family. Rituals have been understood by anthropologists and sociologists as performing important functions; forging a sense of belonging amongst members of a society, delineating who is in and who is out, condensing shared beliefs into simplified, symbolic forms. The particularity of family rituals and practices becomes acutely felt when we try to adopt a ritual belonging to another family, who we think are better than us at this kind of thing.

Attempts to create new rituals from without invariably fail because they have not arisen organically from the personalities and interactions of our own specific family. Authentic family rituals arise more often from the quirks of our children than from the intentions of us as parents. A child mispronouncing something is adopted as the way the whole family says that word, a meal gone awry gives a name to that dish for ever. Repetition and rituals seem to intrinsically appeal to children, and when children arrive, we find ourselves creating these playful family moments spontaneously and unself-consciously. Compare this richness to the official parenting advice to 'talk, cuddle, read, play, listen'. Such imperatives, generalised to all families, necessarily sound dead and joyless.

Many parents complain about the negative impact on family life of the obligation schools now impose on parents to listen to their children read aloud every night and to record this in a diary to be submitted to the teacher. In my own experience, exhausted children are forced to read dull school books aloud, rather than cuddling up for a bedtime story or a bit of television time. Mothers or fathers feel obliged to behave as teachers, correcting the child, pushing them to get to the end of the prescribed chapter of the prescribed reading book, rather than as mums and dads, relaxing after work. Unsurprisingly, any child who is struggling to read, finds these sessions unbearably pressurised, as the child's failure is exposed not only at school, but also at home, which no longer offers respite from the demands of the school day where work must be done and rules must be obeyed. Making a particular kind of parent–child interaction a daily obligation, with the demand that the parent account for themselves in the reading diary, has a corrosive effect on family relations and undermines a love of reading. It also causes resentment rather than trust between parents and teachers. The attempt to impose routines within the home from without, based on an external imperative (of improving the child's Standardised Attainment Tests (SATs) score, the school's Office for Standards in Education, Children's Services and Skills (OFSTED) rating and ultimately the nation's educational levels) sets off a destructive dynamic within the family and between home and school.

Sapping Parental Authority

Of course the dynamic of the parent–child relationship is not just founded on fun, closeness and love. The parent–child relationship is not one of equals, for the parent knows that they are tasked with delivering the child safely into adulthood and into the world at large. This responsibility is embedded within our familial interactions, sometimes obliging us to override our spontaneous feelings of pleasure, love or anger in order to do what's best for the child: sending them to bed even though they are having a good time, pretending to be angry to discourage them from dangerous or undesirable behaviour or restraining our fury to keep them safe from our greater size and strength.

Even rituals which do not seem to be mutually pleasurable, such as the rituals of discipline, are nevertheless specific to particular families. The mother who rattles the kitchen drawer containing the punitive wooden spoon, disperses naughty children in all directions, not through terror but through a ritual, half fun, half acceptance of maternal authority. The verbal rituals of 'wait till your father gets home', 'don't let your mother hear you say that' or 'because I say so!' are subtle reminders and enforcements of family roles and family rules, of parental solidarity and authority. However, one of the most fundamental aims of parenting support is to train out of us, anything other than one type of discipline: positive parenting. All official parenting advice proscribes smacking and shouting as unhelpful or even damaging to children. Inevitably, anti-smacking campaigners claim that physical chastisement is damaging to children's brains, equating physical abuse and trauma with the everyday parenting of raised voices and smacks on the bottom (Burke 2000; New Scientist 2009).

Helen Reece's close analysis of the development of the positive parenting imperative in official parenting literature offers many insights concerning the position into which parents are now placed by official advice (2013). The precepts of positive parenting are that there should be no punishment, only 'positive reinforcement' of good behaviour, parents must set a good example to their child (no hitting or shouting) and they must always respect the child. The child's bad behaviour is understood entirely as the product of parental mistakes or misunderstandings of the child's point of view. Positive reinforcement means that the parent must always be on the lookout for good behaviour which they can praise. Smacking or shouting is interpreted as a sign that the parent has lost control and they must apologise to the child. What parents might understand to be the exercise of parental authority is therefore reinterpreted by experts as a moment where legitimate parental authority is negated or lost.

As Reece points out, positive parenting is an expansive and demanding task which requires constant vigilance and 'attunement' to the child, but it also puts the parent at a distance, cooling their spontaneous reactions to the child's behaviour and adopting a professionalised stance of behaviour management. Yet, UK parents continue to express ambivalent attitudes towards physical chastisement. Some surveys indicate that 80 % of Brits believe in smacking, while others put the figure as much lower, only a third of parents. A 2012 poll found 63 % of Britons were opposed to banning smacking while another reported that 48 % of parents still 'admit' to smacking but few would see it as good or ideal parenting.

Over recent years, alternative rituals of discipline have become visible amongst British parents, and these follow the behaviour management rather than the direct disciplinary model. Back in 2004, the 'Supernanny' television series prompted many parents to try 'the naughty step' on their own children (a version of 'time-out') and it is rare to go into a family home today without seeing a half-filled star-chart stuck to the fridge or a jar of pasta 'rewards' on the windowsill. These tricks of child management, which require the child to 'reflect' on bad behaviour or the parent to reward the good, seem to have become incorporated into our family practices (Bristow 2009). But rituals of discipline can only work when they are inhabited by genuine, spontaneous parental will. Hearing a parent repeat in a dead voice, the mantras, 'you won't get a sticker if you do that', 'that is not acceptable behaviour' or 'use your words', whilst the child continues blithely with whatever they were doing, is a familiar scene. Discipline is only effective when children think we mean it, and that is when we have decided that enough is enough, not when we go through the motions of enacting 'effective parenting strategies', borrowed from an expert.

Professionalising Parenting

The message from parenting support services to all parents is that parenting requires expert knowledge. Being a 'good parent' becomes being what Vansieleghem calls the 'learning parent' (2010, p. 345); this is a requirement without end because 'parental expertise (in terms of competencies) is not only something one should have, but something the parent can never have enough of. It is something in which the parent must invest to make parenting ever more successful' (p. 349). However, good neuroparenting is not just about acquiring knowledge and practicing skills, it is about developing an emotional disposition and a level of commitment to observing, 'reading' and interacting with the child in an instrumental way, which echoes the 'positive parenting' approach. While attachment has been understood as specifically important in a particular period of a child's development, attunement is a process without end; after all, the child will be changing day by day, even minute by minute, if their brain is developing. It is an imperative without limits: there is always room for improvement when it comes to being a sensitive parent. Training parents to monitor and alter their emotional disposition is even more intrusive than trying to get them to adopt star-charts instead of smacking. It is also far more likely to increase parental anxiety; we can all decide that a star chart isn't working and try something else, but can we so easily reject the claim that our own emotional baggage is what is causing problems for our child?

Normalising Help-Seeking

For all the talk of the early days, months and years being the most difficult and the most important, the imperative to seek support to become a more sensitive parent never ends, because children's needs change as they develop. Different experts and authorities therefore pop up at different stages to claim their moment in the parent training sun. Increasingly, neuroparenting experts seek to insert themselves into the parenting of teenagers, with books such as 'Blame My Brain: the Amazing Teenage Brain Revealed' (Morgan 2013), 'The Teenage Brain: A Neuroscientist's Survival Guide to Raising Adolescents and Young Adults' (Jensen and Nutt 2016) and 'Brainstorm: The Power and Purpose of the Teenage Brain' (Siegel 2014). The claim that the brain does not fully mature until the age of 25 (Wallis 2013) has become a truism of contemporary parenting culture that we haven't time to explore here, but it was in some ways presaged in the prioritising of the 'teenage pregnancy problem' in New Labour policy from the late 1990s. Teenage pregnancy was reframed from a moral problem of sex to a social problem of the production and reproduction of inadequate parents. The high-profile teenage pregnancy strategy was a forum through which many of the arguments for parenting support were forged (Macvarish 2010; Macvarish and Billings 2010; Koffman 2014). Programmes of intensive parenting and relationship support for young, 'vulnerable' mothers were therefore established, including the Family Nurse Partnership, a programme brought (and bought) over from the USA, where it operates as the Nurse Family Partnership. Given the current emphasis on 'parenting support for all', it seems that, at least in the eyes of policy-makers, we are all vulnerable 'teenage' parents now.

Institutionalised neuroparenting stresses that new knowledge means 'we now know' how important parenting is in the early years. The parent appears to be exalted as the all-determining presence in the child's journey to adulthood. But, by the exacting standards of neuroparenting, even the best parents cannot get it right 'enough' all of the time, thus creating space for the claim that experts, informed by neuroscience, have greater authority than parents when it comes to knowing what is best for children.

One proposal of the 1001 Critical Days manifesto is designed to inculcate help-seeking behaviour in parents from the very beginning. At present, UK parents must register their baby's arrival at a local Registry Office within 42 days of the birth. Parents are not legally obliged to do anything other than this until they are required by law to see that their children are educated either in a school or via alternative, approved arrangements. They are not obliged to engage with children's services, to allow a midwife or health visitor into their home, or to send their child to pre-school. But the 1001 Critical Days advocates want to nationalise an experiment in which birth registration can be done at Children's Centres.

Since 2001, Benchill Sure Start Centre in Manchester has offered birth registration. The public rationale for the initiative was convenience; it would save new parents a trip to a more distant public office. Behind the scenes however, there was a hope that it would provide an opportunity to 'engage' fathers, but even more significantly, the scheme is now lauded for operationalising 'a key lever in engaging with all families—particularly those that are deemed "hard to reach"—because everyone has a legal obligation to register their baby'. What this has meant at the Benchill Centre is that staff have 'taken the opportunity to register families automatically for Sure Start during their visit, and also provide information about all the Sure Start services in the area'. However well-meaning the local staff may be, this represents an atrocious exploitation of the legal requirement to register a birth in order to 'lever' parents into registering with parent training services. It also creates an opportunity for state employees to gather data about parental circumstances, which will then be shared with other services, increasing the net of monitoring and surveillance that surrounds parents in poorer areas (All Party Parliamentary Sure Start Group 2013).

If the institutionalised norm of good parenting requires an acceptance of the universal need for parenting support, how is the parent who does not wish to 'engage' regarded? Are they judged to be self-sufficient and content to sort things out for themselves or are they problematised as 'hard to reach'? Are they confident in their own abilities or do they have something to hide? The autonomous parent who feels that they know best how to raise their child and who values the privacy of family life, is thus pathologised as being ignorant of the true challenges of parenthood and failing to recognise the need for official intervention. Maggie Mellon, vice chair of the British Association of Social Workers, has recently warned that 'suspicion of parents and of families has become corrosive' in social work, with one in 20 families in England and Wales now investigated for child abuse despite there being 'no significant rise in the number of children who die as a result of parental abuse or neglect' (Mellon 2016).

Exploiting the Transition to Parenthood

The 'transition to parenthood' is increasingly talked up as a difficult process which requires support from without. It is not just that women need specialist maternity care during pregnancy and labour for the sake of their own health, but that they must be supported to become good mothers for the sake of the child (Lowe et al. 2015). Their good motherhood must begin from conception (and even before) with attentive care of the foetus. The amount of advice from all quarters is staggering and it is not just addressed to mothers. According to UNICEF's 'Building A Happy Baby' leaflet for parents-to-be, all family members should pay attention to the 'bump':

> During pregnancy, your baby's brain is growing very quickly and you can help this growth by taking some time out to relax and talk to him, to stroke your bump and maybe play some music to him. Encourage other close family members to do the same. (UNICEF 2014)

In West London, the Chelsea and Westminster NHS Foundation Trust has launched 'womb song' workshops in which mothers-to-be are encouraged to sing to their foetus to 'positively influence the parent-child bond' and 'facilitate language development' (ChelWest 2012). In Newcastle, future parents can take part in what is called a 'fun, interactive and informative course' designed to show 'what you can do right now during pregnancy to help your baby to be happy and grow into a confident resilient child. Becoming a parent is at once one of life's greatest rewards and challenges' (Newcastle 2016). The uncertainty, trepidation and excitement many women and men will inevitably feel when facing the prospect of becoming parents, especially today when so much significance is loaded onto it, is exploited as a 'window of opportunity' to 'engage' them with parenting support services, and to establish the help-seeking habit. To establish this norm, the transition to parenthood is talked up as inherently problematic; the need for support is to be expected:

> Pregnancy, birth and the first 24 months can be tough for every mother and father, and some parents may find it hard to provide the care and attention their baby needs. But it can also be a chance to affect great change, as pregnancy and the birth of a baby is a critical 'window of opportunity' when parents are especially receptive to offers of advice and support. (1001 Critical Days 2013, p. 5)

Such 'expert' voices repeatedly warn parents how difficult it is to become good, happy parents (in particular with the prospect of depression being raised at every opportunity). Parents are told just how vital their behaviour and attitude is to their child's long-term well-being and are strongly guided towards 'sharing the journey' with multiple professionals. What is not spelt out is that as well as offering advice, all of these new-style professionals have an obligation to share concerns amongst themselves and to 'report them up' to old-style state authorities in the form of social services and, ultimately, to the police. They are not, therefore, neutral sources of 'support', however well-meaning staff intend to be, and however much the facilities and information on offer may prove to be useful. Perhaps the so-called 'hard-to-reach' realise this, which is why they remain reluctant to put themselves under the watchful eyes of parenting support services.

New Rituals for Old

Child psychologist Jerome Kagan suggests that there is something reassuring about thinking we can control the path from the present to the future through moulding the child. He describes how the belief in parental determinism gives rise to 'rationalized, ritual practices', which help to sweep away some of the worry associated with this incredible responsibility and 'absorb anxiety like a sponge' (Kagan 1998, pp. 85–86). In a similar vein, Nadesan proposes that 'brain science' functions as a form of 'ritual magic', ensuring the optimisation of infant potential as 'idealized entrepreneurial subjects' (Nadesan 2002, p. 401). In Chap. 3, we discussed how Diane Eyer likened the practice of placing newborns on their mothers' chests for 'skin-to-skin' contact to 'magical thinking', promising to 'inoculate' the baby from harm. However, although the new rituals of neuroparenting—instrumentalised talking, singing, cuddling, reading, playing and so on—seem to offer the hope of controlling the precarious process of child development, there is little evidence to suggest that they are effective at absorbing parental or societal anxiety in any lasting way. This 'mommy blogger' demonstrates that the intensity of attention and the degree of acquired knowledge, required to be a good neuroparent continually expands. She describes enacting the 'serve and return' ritual:

> Baby loves it when you mimic her facial expressions, coo at her little sounds and gaze into her eyes. When baby tries to engage with you in one of those ways, she needs you to respond in kind. This 'serve and return' interaction is foundational in wiring baby's brain. It helps the brain develop in a way that supports stress regulation, empathy and emotional stability. Brain imaging shows that it also activates the pleasure center in baby's brain. (Cutchlow 2015)

But proactive stimulation is not enough and may even be harmful, because the truly sensitive parent needs to know that 'sometimes, baby needs a break':

> I was leaning over my newborn on a play mat, laughing and cooing, when baby suddenly turned her head to the left, lost in a million-mile stare. I had an urge to say, 'Hello? Where'd you go?' Then I remembered that when a baby is overstimulated, she tells you by turning her head away, closing her eyes, avoiding your gaze, tensing up, or suddenly becoming fussy. It was neat for me to understand what was happening. And it helped me resist my initial urge to bring baby back by calling her name or waving in front of her face. My baby turned back to me just a few moments later, ready to carry on. Matching baby's lulls by patiently waiting and then engaging when she does is a hallmark of responsive, sensitive parenting. You're attuned to baby, aware of baby's cues and quick to respond to baby's cues. Sensitive parenting helps baby form a trusting relationship with you, called 'secure attachment'. (Cutchlow 2015)

This mother seems to derive satisfaction from becoming a lay expert in neurodevelopment, echoing Charlotte Faircloth's finding that mothers who fully embraced the scientific 'correctness' of 'attachment parenting' did so because it enabled them to manage their identity as highly educated women who were devoting themselves, full-time, to caring for their baby (Faircloth 2010, 2013). However, with so much invested in being a good mother and with the belief that the child embodies the quality and commitment of this maternal nurture, it is not difficult to see that there is also the potential for much anxiety and disappointment should things not go to plan (Kukla 2008).

In contrast to the intensively conscious, highly active, maternal care is the so-called 'still-face paradigm'. This was an experiment devised by the psychologist Ed Tronick in 1975, to test whether infants are instigators of parental interaction. Babies were filmed reacting as their mothers began by talking and playing with them at close quarters but then suddenly adopted an expressionless 'still face'. The babies first tried to re-engage the mother but became distressed and then resigned as their actions fail to produce the desired response. The 'still-face paradigm' has now become more than just a laboratory experiment; in neuroparenting discourse, it is invoked as an apocryphal tale, warning mothers of the need to be continually responsive to their baby's 'cues'. For health visitors and other professionals, it serves as an emotive reminder to scrutinise new mothers for signs of post-natal depression, which they believe may endanger the child's neurobiological development.

Parenting interventions have been devised which involve filming parents interacting with their babies (as Tronick did) and playing back the recording to the parent while a professional interprets the relationship dynamics and encourages the mother to reflect on the impact of her demeanour. Those who advocate such 'reflective' parenting sometimes do so in opposition to parenting classes which teach parenting as a set of skills. This sounds more democratic and empowering—teaching parents how to reflect on their own parenting, rather than getting them to robotically adopt techniques from external authorities. But this micro-scrutiny from without is aimed at creating perfectly sensitive parents from within. This is called by some parenting experts, being 'mind-minded' (Meins et al. 2012) and this too has been turned into a parent training programme called 'Parenting in Mind' (NSPCC 2016). We can see from the mummy blogger analysing her own interactions that this is a way of caring for babies that requires continual, intense, critical, self-scrutiny. It is difficult to imagine this as being anything other than fraught with anxiety. The intention to inculcate a way of parenting that claims to have 'preventative mental health' properties for babies, therefore, may in fact contribute to the 'perfect madness' of intensive parenting culture for their mothers (Warner 2006).

Bowlby's WHO report stated that a baby requires a 'warm, intimate, and continuous relationship with his mother' (1952, p. 13). But we are a long way from this relatively simple claim that babies need a mother figure to whom they can attach and who can make them feel secure. Attached and attuned neuroparenting is highly intensive, emotionally fraught, requires the engagement of expertise, and an acceptance of scrutiny by those who claim to have expertise and are often in positions of authority. The institutionalisation of an intensive style of parenting goes far beyond encouraging parents to read to their children or take them to museums at the weekend to build cultural capital. It gets into the very hearts and minds of the family by reconstructing the raising of children as a risky, endlessly demanding task which ultimately falls entirely on the shoulders of parents, and particularly, of mothers. However, while responsibility for child outcomes is entirely privatised to parenting, the intimate, privatised, parental performance is assumed to be of the utmost public import. As Gillies and Edwards warn, 'the boundary between 'private families' and 'public concerns' has shifted recently' and whereas family 'and the minutiae of everyday domestic life were previously, at least rhetorically, regarded as separate and protected from public intrusion, or at least only subject to broad-brush policies and state intervention in extreme cases', they are now posed 'as a site of uncertainty and ignorance, especially in relation to rearing and caring for children', which legitimises a whole new level of intrusive state action (Edwards and Gillies 2012, p. 66).

Undermining Parental Love

Families raise children into a world, not just through 'practices' and emotional dispositions, but through beliefs they hold in common with others about adulthood and childhood. While it might be true that these beliefs are more diverse and individualised than before, the legacy of modernity in Britain is that most of us still find babies cute and lovable; we don't disapprove of adults playing with infants; we think that it is a good thing for adults and children to share mealtimes at least some of the time; that children settle down to sleep in their own beds with a teddy and a bedtime story, and we assume that parents are entitled to discipline their children. While these beliefs are held in common, they are enacted by each family in its own way. The institutionalisation of neuroparenting risks overriding an existing culture that is essentially supportive of intimacy and family relations, and replacing it with one that has the opposite effect. Making parents accountable to external, long-term outcomes, measurable in the child's achievements or even in their brain, threatens to undermine the unconditional, spontaneous love that parents provide not because the Prime Minister or professional play adviser tells them it matters, but because they feel it.

This new cultural imperative affects all parent–child relationships as it is so thoroughly entrenched in all the institutions with which parents are obliged to interact: midwives, health visitors, GPs, nursery school staff, childminders and school teachers. The balance between loving our children unconditionally, doing what's best for them, caring for them, while also disciplining them, is a complicated set of choices to negotiate. Walking this path is made no easier by the dogmatic, simplistic message that is increasingly the one we most encounter. This all raises the serious question: if baby care and child-rearing are no longer intimate pleasures and parents are no longer unique and special, why would parents continue to undertake this endeavour? What's in it for them?

References

All Party Parliamentary Sure Start Group. (2013). *Best practice for a Sure Start: The way forward for children's centres.* London: 4Children.

Bowlby, J. (1995 [1952]). *Maternal care and mental health.* Lanham: Jason Aronson Inc.

Bristow, J. (2009). *Standing up to supernanny.* Exeter: Imprint Academic.

Bristow, J. (2016). *The sociology of generations: New directions and challenges.* London: Palgrave Macmillan.

Burke, J. (2000, December 31). Harsh words can deform children's brains for life. *The Guardian.*

ChelWest. (2012). Innovative singing workshops for pregnant women are back, website, 25 Apr 2012. http://www.chelwest.nhs.uk/about-us/news/news-archive/2012/innovative-singing-workshops. Accessed 12 Jan 2016.

Cutchlow, T. (2015). How to read your newborn's cues. Blog, www.huffingtonpost.com/tracy-cutchlow/how-to-read-your-newborns-cues_b_6725586.html. Accessed 12 Jan 2016.

Daly, M., & Bray, R. (2015). Parenting support in England: The bedding down of a new policy. *Social Policy and Society, 14*(04), 633–644.

Edwards, R., & Gillies, V. (2012). Farewell to family? Notes on an argument for retaining the concept. *Families Relationships and Societies, 1*(1), 63–69.

Faircloth, C. (2010). "If they want to risk the health and well-being of their child, that's up to them": Long-term breastfeeding, risk and maternal identity. *Heath, Risk and Society, 12*(4), 357–367.

Faircloth, C. (2013). *Militant lactivism? Infant feeding and maternal accountability in the UK and France.* Oxford/New York: Berghahn Books.

Jensen, F. E., & Nutt, A. E. (2016). *The teenage brain: A neuroscientist's survival guide to raising adolescents and young adults.* New York: Harper Collins.

Kagan, J. (1998). *Three seductive ideas.* Cambridge/London: Harvard University Press.

Koffman, O. (2014). Fertile bodies, immature brains?: A genealogical critique of neuroscientific claims regarding the adolescent brain and of the global fight against adolescent motherhood. *Social Science & Medicine, 143*, 255–261.

Kukla, R. (2008). Measuring motherhood. *The International Journal of Feminist Approaches to Bioethics, 1*(1), 67–90.

Lowe, P., Lee, E., & Macvarish, J. (2015). Growing better brains? Pregnancy and neuroscience discourses in English social and welfare policies. *Health, Risk and Society, 17*, 15–29.

Macvarish, J. (2010). The effect of "risk-thinking" on the contemporary construction of teenage motherhood. *Health Risk & Society, 12*(4), 313–322.

Macvarish, J., & Billings, J. (2010). Challenging the irrational, amoral and antisocial construction of the 'teenage mother'. In S. Duncan, R. Edwards, &

C. Alexander (Eds.), *Teenage parenting—What's the problem?* London: Tufnell Press.

Meins, E., Fernyhough, C., de Rosnay, M., Arnott, B., Leekam, S. R., & Turner, M. (2012). Mind-mindedness as a multidimensional construct: Appropriate and nonattuned mind-related comments independently predict infant–mother attachment in a socially diverse sample. *Infancy, 17*(4), 393–415.

Mellon, M. (2016, February 19). Have parents become the enemy in social work? *Community Care.* http://www.communitycare.co.uk/2016/02/19/parents-become-enemy-social-work/?cmpid=NLC%7CSCSC%7CSC019-2016-0225. Accessed 19 Feb 2016.

Morgan, N. (2013). *Blame my brain: The amazing teenage brain revealed.* London: Walker Books.

Nadesan, M. H. (2002). Engineering the entrepreneurial infant: Brain science, infant development toys, and governmentality. *Cultural Studies, 16*(3), 401–432.

National Literacy Trust. (2005). Why do many young children lack basic language skills? http://www.literacytrust.org.uk/assets/0000/1151/discussionpaper.pdf

New Scientist. (2009, September 25). Smacking hits kids' IQ. https://www.newscientist.com/article/dn17856-smacking-hits-kids-iq/

Newcastle. (2016). Happy babies. http://newcastlepregnancyandbabycentre.co.uk/services.php?p=Happy_Babies. Accessed 17 Jan 2016.

NSPCC. (2016). Pregnancy in mind. https://www.nspcc.org.uk/services-and-resources/services-for-children-and-families/pregnancy-in-mind/. Accessed 10 Jan 2016.

Reece, H. (2013). The pitfalls of positive parenting. *Ethics and Education, 8*(1), 42–54.

Siegel, D. (2014). *Brainstorm: The power and purpose of the teenage brain.* New York: TarcherPerigee.

Unicef. (2014). Building a happy baby: A guide for parents. http://www.unicef.org.uk/Documents/Baby_Friendly/Leaflets/building_a_happy_baby.pdf. Accessed 12 Jan 2016.

Vansieleghem, N. (2010). The residual parent to come: On the need for parental expertise and advice. *Educational Theory, 6*(3), 341–355.

Wallis, L. (2013, September 23). Is 25 the new cut-off point for adulthood?. *BBC News Online.* http://www.bbc.co.uk/news/magazine-24173194. Accessed 15 Jan 2016.

Warner, J. (2006). *Perfect madness, motherhood in the age of anxiety.* London: Vermilion.

CHAPTER 6

The Problem with Neuroparenting

Abstract Neuroparenting persists despite numerous critiques of its claims. Macvarish draws out the consequences of this new way of thinking about how parents ought to relate to their children. Because neuroparenting involves scientific expertise in the translation of babies' needs, the parent is necessarily demoted. Mothers in particular are placed under considerable pressure to conform to this new idea of intensive motherhood: doing more and doing it earlier. The child is conceptualised in deterministic terms as the product of their parents' love and care and in depersonalised, dehumanising terms, as the embodiment of parental 'inputs' rather than as a unique individual. Family life is reinterpreted as a place of risk but also a place where the instrumental task of improving 'outcomes' by increasing parental 'input' takes place. The undermining of lay knowledge and familial and community experience, combined with the churn in professional advice has a potentially disorienting effect. The unique rewards derived from the spontaneity of family relationships risk being diminished by the imposition of external imperatives on the parent–child relationship.

Keywords Neuroparenting • Neuroscience • Neurosceptic • Expertise • Authority • Parenting • Childhood • Intensive motherhood • Family • Risk • Instrumentalisation

Since the late 1990s, there have been serious attempts to challenge and correct the brain-claims made by the first three years movement. Starting with Jerome Kagan (1998) and John Bruer (1999) in the USA, a substantial international body of academic critique has been built (see Macvarish et al. 2014). Scholars in the sciences have challenged the movement's interpretation of scientific data and its tendency towards rigid infant determinism. They have argued against the movement's insistence that the early years are 'critical' in a now-or-never sense, countering that in fact the human brain is defined by its plasticity rather than its rigidity and human development is marked by resilience rather than vulnerability (Belsky and de Haan 2011; Blakemore 2000; Bruer 1997, 1998a, b, 1999; Kagan 1998; Rutter 2002, 2011; Thompson and Nelson 2001). Belsky and de Haan's 2011 review of the latest evidence on the influence of parenting on child brain development concluded, 'The study of parenting and brain development is not even yet in its infancy; it would be more appropriate to conclude that it is still in the embryonic stage, if not that which precedes conception' (Belsky and Haan 2011, p. 410). Sarah-Jayne Blakemore's review of the 0–3 evidence, commissioned by the Parliamentary Office for Science and Technology in 2000, when the House of Commons was considering what was needed in the provision of early years education, cautioned:

> Although babies' brains undergo a large amount of change in the first few years of life, parts of the human brain continue to develop well into adolescence and beyond. Even the adult brain is capable of change. It is therefore difficult to make direct links from the neuroscientific evidence to specific early childhood environments, experiences and early child-care policies. (Blakemore 2000, p. 5)

This book has drawn on these reviews of the scientific evidence but also sought to expand the critique emerging from the social sciences and the humanities of the movement's foundational presumptions; intensive parenting and parental determinism (notably the work of Val Gillies, Ros Edwards and Nicola Horsley, Glenda Wall, Linda Blum, Sue White, David Wastell and Brid Featherstone, Deborah Lupton, Frank Furedi and my colleagues at the Centre for Parenting Culture Studies at the University of Kent). Journalists in the UK have occasionally picked up on the academic discourse and investigated further the reach of brain-claiming in early years policy and child protection (Williams 2014; Butler 2014); this has, in turn, been relayed back to the USA (see 'Can Brain Science Be

Dangerous?', North 2014). Recent research suggests that this critical discourse is audible to policy-makers and, to some extent, influences their thinking (Broer and Pickersgill 2015a, b).

However, it is clear that despite these criticisms of the claims, suppositions and effects of neuroparenting, the first three years movement has continued to gain ground in the UK and internationally. It has also grown in strength despite a lack of evidence for parental demand for parent training, neuro or otherwise. While parents may well wish for information and advice about specific problems regarding their children, they do not appear to accept the value of generalised parenting support provided by government. Sure Start has been beset by the problem of a relatively low take-up by the very families it was designed to reach (Belsky et al. 2007) and, as discussed in our first chapter, the CANparent trial engaged only 4 % of its target parents. Meanwhile, in a rare example of active resistance to the parenting support agenda, a group of parents in Scotland are currently engaged in the 'NO2NP' campaign against the Scottish government's proposal to assign to every child a state-named professional 'guardian', or Named Person, tasked with overseeing the child's interests from birth (Waiton 2016). All of this suggests a significant 'lack of fit' between what families think they need and what policy-makers think is good for children (Statham and Smith 2010). Nevertheless, the drive to early intervention and parent training has proved to be resilient. Even when programmes of intervention are evaluated as failures or of limited success (see the Family Nurse Partnership evaluation by Robling et al. 2016), the conclusion drawn is that more needs to be done to help parents recognise the benefits of such services or practitioners need to reach babies even earlier.

Presumed Helplessness

Throughout the first three years movement, there is a presumption that people cannot improve their circumstances by themselves, even though studies suggest that families often get themselves out of challenging situations by recourse to their own networks of support (Statham and Smith 2010). In a recent survey conducted by Mumsnet, it was found that the source of non-medical support and advice judged to be most useful by mothers who had experienced post-natal depression, was that offered by a partner and close friends (Mumsnet 2015). The survey also found that 54 % of mothers who had sought professional support for post-natal depression had been worried 'that having a diagnosis would raise concerns about my ability to care for my child' and 42 % were concerned 'that healthcare professionals would judge me'. This suggests that despite their best efforts at destigmatising help-seeking behaviour, maternal and child health professionals have failed to convince many people that state services are safe or non-judgemental. Research with early years practitioners in Australia indicates that training in neuroparenting has provided grounds for the pre-judgement and surveillance of mothers, as indicated by this family support social worker; 'So it is pretty much a given if mum's got mental health issues, if she is not feeding the baby properly there's every good chance she's also got issues going around attachment because she is not cueing in' (Lawless et al. 2013, p. 426).

Parents may well find it difficult to trust professionals when they know that one possible option, should concerns arise about their parenting, is the permanent removal of their children from their care. There is increasing concern that in adoption policy, the imperative to intervene early, in the name of preventing neuroemotional damage, has been used to speed up the forced removal of children from birth parents (Featherstone et al. 2013; Wastell and White 2012; White and Wastell 2015). Professor of social work, Sue White, reports that in 2015, the UK was criticised by the Council of Europe for its practice of allowing adoption without the consent of the birth parents. The number removed by so-called 'forced adoption' in the UK in 2013 was 3020; this contrasted with just 250 in Germany in 2010 (Council of Europe 2015). Critical social work professionals have implicated brain determinism in creating a 'rhetorical potency' through its 'now or never' argument, which legitimises a 'drive towards early removal and has become a powerful and unquestioned professional mantra' (Featherstone et al. 2013, p. 5). They cite as evidence a statement by the President of the Association of Directors of Children's Services (on Radio 4's Today programme on 10 February 2012) explaining that the significant increase in care orders was due to a 'better understanding of the effect of neglectful parenting due to drug and alcohol problems and the physical damage to development and to brain development it can do with very young children' (Featherstone et al. 2013, p. 5). This 'hard end' of neuroparenting should be of great concern to us all. Others in the field of social work raise concerns that the emphasis on risk prevention and on predicting and preventing 'emotional harm' has led to unprecedented numbers of UK families being subject to surveillance and intervention.

The intentions of the operators within the first three years movement are often benevolent; they wish to improve the lives of children, support parents and solve some of the most serious problems facing society. But good intentions can result in extremely negative unintended consequences and they can be rationalised by wrong-headed ideas which move us further away from truth and understanding. We have to consider that in the process of attempting to strengthen society by intervening in the relationships between parents and their children, neuroparenting and the drive to manage from without the earliest years of parenthood potentially strip family life of what makes it meaningful. Family relationships are only meaningful insofar as they are unique to us as sets of individuals, tied together by spontaneous bonds of dependence, love and care. Without the privacy necessary to experience these bonds unself-consciously and to build within them the special meanings unique to our family, raising children ceases to be pleasurable or fulfilling.

Studies of the influence of neurothinking more broadly indicate that neuroparenting is likely to be received and interpreted across the general public in a highly mediated way, working with existing and competing ways of thinking, being rejected and reconstituted (Pickersgill 2013). But given that neuroparenting seems to have taken such a hold amongst opinion-formers, certain professional groups, policy-makers and policy-practitioners, we should pay close attention to whether and how it plays out with the parenting public. There is, so far, a relatively small amount of research about the specific impact of brain-claims on how parents think about what they do, but what there is, supports the argument that neuroparenting is the most concentrated form of intensive parenting, with a strong presumption of parental determinism (Lupton 2011; Romagnoli and Wall 2012; Wall 2004, 2010). We will now consider how neuroparenting further disseminates and entrenches these presumptions.

Further Intensifying Motherhood

There is plenty of evidence from sociological research that parents have internalised some of the norms of intensive parenting conveyed through parenting culture (Hays 1996; Ennis 2014; Lee 2007a, b). If we return to the Mumsnet survey referred to above, we get an indication of the effect of intensive motherhood on mothers. Asked what contributed to their Postnatal Depression (PND), 65 % of the respondents named the 'pressure to be "the perfect mother"' and 46 %, the 'pressure to bond with your baby and/or to feel overwhelming love for them'. Twenty-nine per cent considered 'The pressure to breastfeed, from other people' a significant factor, while 48 % blamed their own expectations of breastfeeding (Mumsnet 2015). It is tempting to draw the conclusion that the concerted efforts of the past 15 years to tell mothers just how much they matter to their child's long-term development have made it more, not less, difficult for parents to deal with raising their children.

This comment, taken from an online forum that was part of a training module in neuroparenting for parents and professionals, indicates that some mothers are receptive to claims about the negative effects of stress on the foetus and think they should be pushed more forcefully towards mothers:

> I don't think most expectant mothers do think about the effect stress can have long term on the unborn baby. I really think mothers should be made more aware of this in antenatal appointments. I am currently pregnant and have been careful with food and alcohol during pregnancy as these are things I can easily change. Stress is much harder to control though, I have to work and face stresses there and also have felt stressed about something going wrong with the pregnancy. It does make me realise that I need to not allow things to get to me for the sake of my unborn child's health.

On the same forum, a child care professional said:

> I think society needs to see 'developing baby' rather than 'pregnant woman' so that the baby's needs are prioritised. For example, most people tend to be more mindful of the impact of arguing or stressful situations on a child and will try to protect them from it but because the unborn baby can't be seen in the room, I think they are almost 'forgotten' about. Concerns/queries/conversations tend to focus on how the pregnant woman is feeling (e.g. 'It must be uncomfortable trying to sit/walk/sleep now that you are so big') rather than how the baby is feeling (e.g. 'your baby must be feeling a little squashed now, she's running out of room to move around'). (FutureLearn 2015)

These women were responding to videos on 'toxic stress' produced by the Harvard Center on the Developing Child and their comments indicate the potential problems with imagining ever more threats to the infant brain. The stresses and strains of everyday life become viewed as toxic, mothers feel compelled to continually monitor not just their food and drink intake, but their emotional state, while others feel compelled to monitor mothers. Ultimately, the woman becomes effaced, as she is very much a secondary concern, reduced to the status of a potentially toxic vessel for the developing baby (Armstrong 2003).

The following are all examples of parental worries expressed in online forums: a pregnant woman worries about the moderate levels of alcohol she drank before she realised she was pregnant; a new mother is wracked with guilt about failing to breastfeed; another new mother wonders how to motivate herself to stimulate her baby's brain through talking, singing and playing, when she finds it all pretty boring; a mother, returning to work after maternity leave, is concerned that her baby is not 'securely attached' because he went happily into a stranger's arms at a new nursery; a mother cannot square the idea of group day care with the kind of one-to-one, moment-by-moment responsiveness she thinks babies need; the mother of a toddler is worried that because her child prefers to chew the books she tries to read to him, he is not on the path to being 'school ready'; many, many mothers concerned that they are too 'shouty' with their children or have been tempted to smack and are therefore not 'modelling good behaviour' and are creating a stressful home.

Amongst the new class of parenting experts, there is an unshakeable belief that they are necessary because parents are struggling to cope with everyday life. When it comes to 'ordinary' parents, who are not child murderers, abusers or neglecters, they are most often portrayed as 'lacking in confidence'. Indeed, the contemporary construction of parenting as simultaneously 'the most important job in the world' and 'the most difficult job in the world' means that the raising of children becomes a source of great anxiety. However, all of the worries listed above will play out within the pragmatic realities of daily life: getting a baby fed somehow, the baby becoming more interesting and responsive, going back to work because it's financially necessary, giving the baby a book to chew on and leaving the cultivation of pre-literacy skills for another day, shouting on some days, smacking on others, laughing off bad behaviour when it feels right. It is true to say that being a parent is something we learn 'on the job', but does this mean that it can be taught?

It might seem as though some of the concerns described above could be solved by parent training containing advice about pregnancy, infant feeding and discipline, for example. Practical tips on how to deal with babies and specific advice about health worries can certainly be very helpful to first-time parents. However, the kind of practical, specific advice that comes from medical knowledge and the broad experience of caring for babies is not what is reflected in the imperatives of neuroparenting. The advice that parents must always 'do more' to secure their child's long-term development—abstain pre-emptively from all 'toxic' substances when trying to conceive, persevere with breastfeeding despite pain and lack of milk, talk to and play with even very young babies to make sure they hit their developmental 'milestones', replace shouting and smacking with 'positive parenting'—cannot alleviate the pressures of infant care, they can only intensify them. It seems unlikely that parenting support based on the suppositions of neuroparenting could possibly ease parental anxiety.

All of the evidence suggests that it is mothers who experience the demands of intensive parenting most acutely. Echoing the Mumsnet survey, one academic study found that when mothers were given free rein to talk about their parenting worries, they were primarily concerned with the social pressures which make them feel 'attacked, beleaguered, or unsupported' as they try to 'be the kind of parents they wanted to be' (Hoffmann 2013). The deep internalisation of 'good' motherhood as 'intensive' motherhood meant that raising children was readily experienced as being a fraught process of maternal identity construction, to the extent that '(T)he good child, notably absent as an independent concern, was enmeshed so deeply in aspirations for being a good parent that it had become, for all intents and purposes, invisible' (Hoffmann 2013).

John Gillis observed, back in 1996, that the concept and task of child-rearing had become narrowed to 'mothering', performed primarily by women, with extremely high expectations of maternal commitment. The consequences, he thought, were that some mothers become extremely unforgiving of themselves, '(U)nable to accept their own humanity and the shortcomings this inevitably entails', and leading to 'a disconnection between the idealised motherhood they are expected to live up to and the realities of everyday mothering' (Gillis 1996, p. 178). This worrying development has serious consequences for women's sense of self and their place in the world:

> Modern culture has thus added yet another task to mothers' work; representing herself to herself and to others as something she can never completely be. Never before has this cultural imperative taken up so much space and time in women's lives. Never have mothers been so burdened by motherhood. (Gillis 1996, p. 178)

Developmental psychologist Diane Eyer's study of the attempt to promote mother–infant bonding through skin-to-skin post-natal contact in hospitals drew the conclusion that the intervention left a substantial proportion of women feeling worse about their mothering (1992). Those who had not been able to partake in prolonged skin-to-skin contact because of complications with their health or their babies' were profoundly worried that they had missed a 'window of opportunity' to bond, and therefore had threatened their child's future mental health. According to Eyer, bonding is an 'impossible standard to adhere to', constructed of '(O) verstated imperatives that later prove to be virtually groundless' and, as such, 'cannot enhance trust' between women and professionals involved in maternity care (Eyer 1992, p. 90). She also warned that the bonding imperative may contribute to women having unrealistic expectations of their children and placed an intolerable emotional drain on women and their families.

We should heed these warnings from the front line of intensive parenting and take seriously the implications of further adding to the maternal burden by reifying the significance of mothers' love in the form of the infant brain. We have said little about fathers in this book and that is because for all the gender-neutral connotations of 'parenting', it is primarily mothers to whom neuroparenting addresses itself. However, policy is also continually trying to 'engage fathers', albeit in a much less comprehensive way, and it has been suggested that neuroscience potentially appeals to fathers because it has an objective, non-maternal character. The solution to the problem of intensive motherhood is not to spread it to fathers. As Shirani et al. note (2012), fathers tend to feel less unsure than mothers about their abilities as parents; they are less affected by professional advice and the general questioning of parents' skills. They also focus more on autonomous decision-making, based on notions of instinct or family experience, than on official guidance. This is a positive thing, positioning fathers as potentially able to reduce maternal anxiety and stress, but the more they too are targeted by the neuroparenting message, the less they may be able to fulfil this important role.

While becoming an amateur expert in child development may make parenting more interesting and temporarily boost parental self-confidence, it also threatens to introduce an instability into the parent–child relationship. It has become a truism of contemporary parenting culture that expert advice changes at a remarkably rapid pace. As Eyer points out, 'the history of child-rearing expertise is full of fads and formulas of varying utility' and this churn in parental imperatives potentially confuses us, as we 'increasingly wonder what to believe' (Eyer 1992, p. 90).

What Becomes of the Parent?

As well as being the origin of fundamental social bonds of love and care, family, as a set of intergenerational relationships, has also to be a hierarchy of authority from parent to child. The parent's acceptance of primary responsibility for the care and nurture of their child requires a degree of moral autonomy that inevitably makes them an adult, relative to the child. Their greater experience of life imbues them with a natural authority that has usually been assumed. However, if parents are continually undermined in public discourse and by government action, they risk losing this authority and the autonomy to make their own judgements, and at least in theory, cease to be adults or parents in any real sense. This is the most serious threat posed by neuroparenting (Macvarish et al. 2015). We have a lot more to learn about how its precepts are internalised by parents themselves (or indeed by children), but we know that it is based on a presumption of parental incompetence. According to the new norms, a good parent is one who realises this, accepts their own limitations, recognises the need for expert knowledge and support, and willingly submits to education and training in the love and care of their child (Smeyers 2010; Davis 2010).

What Becomes of the Child?

There seems to be a contradiction between the highly volitional promise of neuro-cultivation and the doom-laden warnings of 'windows of opportunity' slamming shut. While early years determinism suggests that it's all over after 3, or even 2, because the brain is 'set', the culture of intensive parenting simultaneously expands parental obligations to impossible proportions throughout childhood. The two can co-exist because contemporary parenting culture both intensifies and expands the parental role. But not only that, the highly activist agency required of parents, and the naturalised agency of the infant's brain, means that the older child is attributed barely any agency at all. The parent must, therefore continue to provide extremely vigilant care throughout childhood, adolescence and even the early twenties.

The effect of intensive parental cultivation on the child's ability to develop a sense of their own autonomy and to feel responsible for their own emotions, successes and failures are increasingly the subject of speculation, notably in the recent labelling as entitled 'special snowflakes', the young people now entering workplaces and college campuses (Marano 2008). What has been labelled 'over-parenting' or 'helicopter parenting' is an understandable parental response to the heightened sense of risk associated with childhood (Bristow 2014), but are we now beginning to see evidence of the possible outcome of this type of socialisation in the young adults coming of age (Nelson 2010)? Determinism constructs the child as the victim of their parents, what might be the consequence of children believing that their parents have not done enough to nurture their brains?

At an earlier age, if the experience of academic success and failure is framed by beliefs in prior parental input, how does the child understand their struggles with mathematics, for example? Psychologist Carol Dweck's research posits that a belief in hard work rather than natural ability made a positive difference to children's mastery of maths. She uses the brain metaphor in a rather different way to convey her findings and recommends 'instilling a growth mindset' which understands the brain 'as a muscle' which can 'be strengthened through hard work and persistence' (Anderson 2016). We don't need to narrow things down to the brain, however, to appreciate the power of consciousness on our ability to act, as Jerome Kagan put it:

> Both science and autobiography affirm that a capacity for change is as essential to human development as it is to the evolution of new species. The events of the opening years do start an infant down a particular path, but it is a path with an extraordinarily large number of intersections. (Kagan 1998, p. 150)

Besides the possible effects of a belief in parental determinism, concerns have also been expressed about other aspects of our current conceptualisation of children (Lowe et al. 2015). Hennum (2014) argues that in the name of creating 'child-centred' policy, addressing itself to the needs of children in general, the specific, unique child disappears. The child's needs become 'expert-identified' and 'generically defined', while the parent is evaluated, from without, as needing to gain skills and competencies in order to meet them. As evidence of this tendency, Hennum describes how the documents produced in Norwegian child protection cases, 'show a remarkable similarity, despite the fact that they dealt with different girls and boys in a diversity of situations' (2014, p. 451). As a consequence of these generalisations, the 'unique child as a subject of protection seemed to vanish' to be 'replaced by a kind of familiar and uniform mass-produced object, whose life is structured to fit into standardized stories of deviant childhoods' (2014, p. 451). The overall outcome, she warns, 'might be one involving the formation and acceptance of an authoritarian and moralizing state, even a soft totalitarianism' which is 'all done in the name of children' (Hennum 2014, p. 453).

What Becomes of the Family?

The greater the regard given to self-styled parenting experts, the more the parent–child relationship is mediated through external sources of authority. The parent who accepts the precepts of neuroparenting—that their child's brain and future is entirely in their hands, that the quality of their love is 'readable' in the child's brain and that they must do more to secure its development—has also accepted that they do not know best. 'Neuroscience' and its interpreters stand between the child and their parent, protecting the infant brain from uninformed, spontaneous, parental attention. The good neuroparent is one who seeks to manage their child's development and in particular, to manage their child's emotions. This positions the parent as therapist, observing and intervening to steer the child along the correct emotional path. The parents must be in control of themselves at all times in order to control this development. Family relationships are thus reinterpreted along a therapeutic model. Neuroparenting promises to make parental love externalised, observable and measurable but in reality, love has very little to do with neuroparenting or with a therapeutic approach in general. Being your child's therapist or their 'first teacher' is not the same thing as being a parent, this attempt to professionalise the parental role is destructive of the unique character of family relationships.

Recent research with early years workers offers insights into the problem of professionalising relationships of care. Heather Piper et al. (2006) observed that semi-formal settings for adult–child relationships have increasingly restricted touching and holding in the name of professionalised or proceduralised child protection. Verity Campbell-Barr's more recent study compared early years carers from the UK with those from Hungary and asked the question 'where has all the love gone?' (2015). The study's analysis of the English early years curriculum found that talk of emotions has increasingly been excluded in favour of the language of process. The researchers also found that the English students felt that 'policy and procedures' constrained them from being able to respond to the emotional needs of children, particularly when a child was hurt. Although they wanted to provide physical comfort in such circumstances, they felt that this was not appropriate. English carers described feeling that they were no longer able to rock a baby to sleep, or sit a child on their lap because of their training in what constituted professional conduct in early years settings. These findings should serve as a warning about what happens when all those who care for children (including parents) are encouraged to adopt a constrained, 'cooled' stance of emotional detachment and behaviour management.

Parents are increasingly addressed in the same breath as 'other caregivers', with both parties talked of as sharing responsibility for the raising of children; this represents a troubling demotion of parents, but an additional problem is that this is happening within a framework shaped by ideas and practices which seek to limit the spontaneous feelings adults have towards children and to instrumentalise nurturing relationships with the language of input and outcomes.

What Becomes of Community?

We have already highlighted the potentially disorienting effect of the churn in expert thinking about parenting, but Kagan suggests that rapidly changing, external norms also encourage dislocation from the relations of support found within families and communities (Kagan 1998). Vansieleghem highlights the same issue with external intervention's detachment from the social relationships and residual experience of human culture: '(J)ust as traditional norms have in the past, parental services are now normalizing individual behaviour; only these parental services, technologies and monitoring systems are not related to an existing order' (Vansieleghem 2010, p. 354). The invocation of neuroscience in neuroparenting intentionally detaches its advice from existing, lay sources of parental advice and support. The abstractions of nature, science, 'the evidence' or the brain are substituted for advice from old wives' tales or more experienced parents, with the implication that the requirements of neuroparenting float above real-world interests or prejudices. The explicit attack on lived human experience in the name of scientific truth is a dangerous tendency undermining the relationships of support and dependence necessary to human existence, and particularly to the raising of children.

Many have criticised the destructive effects of intensive parenting culture on informal relationships. Highly individualised, competitive parenting strategies and parental tribalism all divide rather than unite parents from one another and from wider adult society. One criticism is that such a culture is unfair; the better-off pass on their privilege by the concerted cultivation of their offspring, while the less wealthy and less educated, fall even further behind. Robert Putnam and others concerned with inequality have identified this problem, but their solution is to inculcate the ways of intensive parenting in all parents. Schemes to get poor mothers talking to their babies are designed to 'level the playing field' of life chances. But it seems naive in the extreme to suppose that deep-rooted inequalities or the problems of economic stagnation could be overcome by parents mechanically reading books to their infants or gazing more intently into their newborn's eyes. Poorer, less-educated parents are still going to be unable to compete once their children reach older childhood and are up against middle-class children whose parents are culturally and socially connected enough to position their children securely within their own milieu and who have the financial resources to buy in private schooling, tuition and extra-curricular activities which further secure the path to higher education and better-paid jobs. To focus on infancy and to focus on parenting is a fundamentally dishonest approach to equalising life chances. It ignores the lack of availability of well-paid jobs, high-quality day care and excellent schooling. The institutionalisation of the expectation that parents 'do more' in pursuit of the false promise of wholly individually determined advancement means that all parents are under increasing pressure to become 'educators' in the narrowest sense.

A Defence of Parental Love

A defence of the family is often assumed to be a conservative project. The argument of this book is that we need to defend the privacy and autonomy which makes family life worth living while also asserting our freedom from the kind of deterministic thinking which makes it impossible for individuals and societies to move forward. The fact of child development means that the parent–child relationship is the most fast-moving of all human relationships, forced continually to rework itself as the dynamics of dependence and independence are played out. To fulfil this intergenerational responsibility, parents need to be supported by adult society as a whole, not told that it's all down to them, while being monitored and evaluated, whether from afar or up-close. Family life may have survived and relatively successfully re-established itself throughout the considerable disruptions of the modern age, but we should seriously question what happens to it when parents are no longer respected as intrinsically the best people to care for children, when the private world of the home is seen as a place of risk and toxicity, and when the path from infancy to adulthood is cast as so precarious from the offset that it may never be left alone to spontaneously occur without expert monitoring and intervention.

Neuroparenting undermines the basis of the relationships of reciprocity at the heart of the family. It holds the parent accountable to the child (or the child's brain), rather than the child to the parent. This is a dangerous overturning of an important social relationship. Precisely because children are always changing and their future is inherently open-ended, they are too unstable to serve as objects of accountability. For parents to live through their child's future is a highly risky identity strategy, precisely because it is beyond our control. At present, we are dangerously close to seeing this strategy writ large, as the way in which adult society seeks to validate itself and move itself forward into the future.

References

Anderson, J. (2016). Stanford professor who pioneered praising effort sees false praise everywhere. http://qz.com/587811/stanford-professor-who-pioneered-praising-effort-sees-false-praise-everywhere/. Accessed 12 Jan 2016.

Armstrong, E. M. (2003). *Conceiving risk, bearing responsibility: Fetal alcohol syndrome and the diagnosis of moral disorder*. Baltimore: The John Hopkins University Press.

Belsky, J., & de Haan, M. (2011). Annual research review. Parenting and children's brain development: The end of the beginning. *Journal of Child Psychology and Psychiatry, 52*(4), 409–428.

Belsky, J., Barnes, J., & Melhuish, E. (2007). *The national evaluation of Sure Start: Does area-based early intervention work?* Bristol: Policy Press.

Blakemore, S. J. (2000). *Early years learning* (POST report). London: Parliamentary Office for Science and Technology.

Bristow, J. (2014). The double bind of parenting culture: Helicopter parents and the cotton wool kids. In E. Lee, J. Bristow, C. Faircloth, & J. Macvarish (Eds.), *Parenting culture studies*. London: Palgrave MacMillan.

Broer, T., & Pickersgill, M. (2015a). Targeting brains, producing responsibilities: The use of neuroscience within British social policy. *Social Science & Medicine, 132*, 54–61.

Broer, T., & Pickersgill, M. (2015b). Low expectations, legitimization, and the contingent uses of scientific knowledge: Engagements with neuroscience in Scottish social policy and services. *Engaging Science, Technology, and Society, 1*, 47–66.

Bruer, J. T. (1997). Education and the brain: A bridge too far. *Educational Researcher, 26*, 4–16.

Bruer, J. T. (1998a). Brain science, brain fiction. *Educational Leadership, 56*(3), 14–18.

Bruer, J. T. (1998b). Time for critical thinking. *Public Health Reports, 113*(5), 389–397.

Bruer, J. (1999). *The myth of the first three years: A new understanding of early brain development and lifelong learning*. New York: The Free Press.

Butler, P. (2014, May 6). Policymakers seduced by neuroscience to justify early intervention agenda. *The Guardian*.

Council of Europe. (2015). Social services in Europe: Legislation and practice of the removal of children from their families in Council of Europe member states. http://website-pace.net/documents/10643/1127812/EDOC_Social+services+in+Europe.pdf/dc06054e-2051-49f5-bfbd-31c9c0144a32. Accessed 12 Feb 2016.

Davis, R. A. (2010). Government intervention in child rearing: Governing infancy. *Educational Theory, 60*(3), 285–298.

Ennis, L. R. (2014). *Intensive mothering: The cultural contradictions of modern motherhood*. Ontario: Demeter Press.

Eyer, D. (1992). *Mother-infant bonding: A scientific fiction*. New Haven/London: Yale University Press.

Featherstone, B., Morris, K., & White, S. (2013). A marriage made in hell: Early intervention meets child protection. *British Journal of Social Work, 44*(7), 1735–1749.

FutureLearn. (2015). Quotes from users of the online course forum 'Babies in Mind'. Accessed 1 Jan 2016.

Gillis, J. R. (1996). *A world of their own making: Myth, ritual, and the quest for family values*. New York: Basic Books.

Hays, S. (1996). *The cultural contradictions of motherhood*. New Haven/London: Yale University Press.

Hennum, N. (2014). Developing child-centered social policies: When professionalism takes over. *Social Sciences, 3*, 441–459.

Hoffmann, D. M. (2013). Raising the awesome child. *IASC: The Hedgehog Review, 15*(3). http://www.iasc-culture.org/THR/THR_article_2013_Fall_Hoffman.php

Kagan, J. (1998). *Three seductive ideas*. Cambridge/London: Harvard University Press.

Lawless, A., Coveney, J., & MacDougall, C. (2013). Infant mental health promotion and the discourse of risk. *Sociology of Health and Illness, 36*(3), 416–431.

Lee, E. (2007a). Health, morality, and infant feeding: British mothers' experiences of formula milk use in the early weeks. *Sociology of Health and Illness, 29*(7), 1075–1090.

Lee, E. (2007b). Infant feeding in risk society. *Health Risk and Society, 9*(3), 295–309.

Lowe, P., Lee, E., & Macvarish, J. (2015). Biologising parenting: Neuroscience discourse, English social and public health policy and understandings of the child. *Sociology of Health and Illness, 37*, 198–211.

Lupton, D. (2011). 'The best thing for the baby': Mothers' concepts and experiences related to promoting their infants' health and development. *Health, Risk & Society, 13*(7–8), 637–651.

Macvarish, J., Lee, E., & Lowe, P. (2014). The 'first three years' movement and the infant brain: A review of critiques. *Sociology Compass, 8*(6), 792–804.

Macvarish, J., Lee, E., & Lowe, P. (2015). Neuroscience and family policy: What becomes of the parent? *Critical Social Policy, 35*(2), 248–269.

Marano, H. (2008). *A nation of wimps: The high cost of invasive parenting.* New York: Crown Publishing Group.

Mumsnet. (2015). Results of postnatal depression survey. http://www.mumsnet.com/surveys/postnatal-depression. Accessed 10 Jan 2016.

Nelson, M. (2010). *Parenting out of control: Anxious parents in uncertain times.* New York/London: New York University Press.

North, A. (2014, November 24). Can brain science be dangerous? *New York Times.* Blog, http://op-talk.blogs.nytimes.com/2014/11/24/can-brain-science-be-dangerous/?smid=fb-share&_r=0. Accessed 10 Jan 2016.

Pickersgill, M. (2013). The social life of the brain: Neuroscience in society. *Current Sociology, 61*, 322.

Piper, H., Powell, J., & Smith, H. (2006). Parents, professionals, and paranoia: The touching of children in a culture of fear. *Journal of Social Work, 6*(2), 151–167.

Robling, M., et al. (2016). Effectiveness of a nurse-led intensive home-visitation programme for first-time teenage mothers (Building Blocks): A pragmatic randomised controlled trial. *Lancet, 387*, 146–155.

Romagnoli, A., & Wall, G. (2012). "I know I'm a good mom": Young, low-income mothers' experiences with risk perception, intensive parenting ideology and parenting education programmes. *Health, Risk and Society, 14*(3), 273–289.

Rutter, M. (2002). Nature, nurture, and development: From evangelism through science toward policy and practice. *Child Development, 73*(1), 1–21.

Rutter, M. (2011, July 11). Interviewed on BBC radio 4 analysis, 'Unsure about Sure Start', transcript of a recorded documentary (p. 6). http://news.bbc.co.uk/nol/shared/spl/hi/programmes/analysis/transcripts/analysis_11_07_11.pdf. Accessed 17 Jan 2016.

Shirani, F., Henwood, K., & Coltart, C. (2012). Meeting the challenges of intensive parenting culture: Gender, risk management and the moral parent. *Sociology, 46*(1), 25–40.

Smeyers, P. (2010). State intervention and the technologization and regulation of parenting. *Educational Theory, 60*(3), 265–270.

Statham, J., & Smith, M. (2010). *Issues in earlier intervention: Identifying and supporting children with additional needs* (Research report). Nottingham: Department for Children, Schools and Families.

Thompson, R. A., & Nelson, C. A. (2001). Developmental science and the media: Early brain development. *American Psychologist, 56*(1), 5–15.

Vansieleghem, N. (2010). The residual parent to come: On the need for parental expertise and advice. *Educational Theory, 6*(3), 341–355.

Waiton, S. (2016). Third way parenting and the creation of the 'Named Person' in Scotland: The end of family privacy and autonomy? SAGEopen.

Wall, G. (2004). Is your child's brain potential maximized?: Mothering in an age of new brain research. *Atlantis, 28*(2), 41–50.

Wall, G. (2010). Mothers' experiences with intensive parenting and brain development discourse. *Women's Studies International Forum, 33*(3), 253–263.

Wastell, D., & White, S. (2012). Blinded by neuroscience: social policy, the family and the infant brain. *Families Relationships and Societies, 1*(3), 397–414.

White, S., & Wastell, D. (2015). The rise and rise of prevention science in UK family welfare: Surveillance gets under the skin. *Families, Relationships and Societies.* http://dx.doi.org/10.1332/204674315X14479283041843

Williams, Z. (2014, April 26). Is misused neuroscience defining early years and child protection policy? *The Guardian.*

Index

A
Abecedarian Program, 73
adolescent brain, 86
adoption, 36, 55, 98
alcohol, 26–7, 98, 100, 101
Allen, Graham M.P., 23, 70
animal studies, 31, 34, 44, 45
Arendt, Hannah, 54
attachment, 9, 15, 20, 42, 44, 46–8, 63, 65, 72, 85, 90, 98
attunement, 9, 84, 85
autism, 28

B
baby ASBOs, 66
Batmanghelidjh, Camila, 11
Bishop, Dorothy, 33
Blair, Tony, 66
bonding, 46–8, 80, 102–3
Bowlby, John, 44, 47, 73, 91
Brazelton, T. Berry, 24–5, 26
breast milk, breastfeeding, 2, 28, 42, 46, 100, 102
Bruer, John, 19–20, 22, 37, 96
Burman, Erica, 23, 36–7, 52–3

C
Cameron, David, 3, 5, 7, 21, 29, 30, 31, 33, 43, 55, 62, 66
CANparent trial, 7–8, 62, 97
Carnegie Corporation, 65
child saving movement, 53
Chua, Amy, 30
Clinton, Bill and Hillary, 65
communication deficit, 80
critical periods, 2, 45-6
crying, 35, 36, 71
cortisol, 2, 35, 70
cycles of deprivation, poverty, disadvantage, 30, 72

D
Davies, Sally, 8
decade of the brain, 19
depression, maternal and paternal, 14, 48
deprived environments, 31, 36
determinism, genetic, parental, emotional, infant, 13, 14, 51, 55–6, 72, 89, 96, 99, 105
Duncan Smith, Iain, MP, 55, 56

E

early intervention, 2, 3, 8, 12, 21, 22, 33, 55, 62, 64, 65, 67, 69, 70, 71, 73, 97
Early Intervention Foundation, 12
Enlightenment, 51, 52
enriched environments, 20, 30–1
eugenics, 53, 54
expertise, 52, 55, 56, 64, 85, 91, 103
Eyer, Diane, 47, 89, 102–3

F

Family Nurse Partnership/Nurse Family Partnership, 73, 86, 97
fathers, 5, 12, 14, 46, 48, 64, 68, 82, 87, 88, 103
Fetal Alcohol Sydnrome, Fetal Alcohol Spectrum Disorder, 26
first three years movement, 6, 11, 20, 21, 22, 23, 27, 30, 42, 43, 46, 51, 56, 57, 61, 65, 68, 73, 78, 96, 97, 99
first years last forever, 6, 12, 20, 21, 23, 62, 63, 65
FrameWorks Institute, 21
From Neurons to Neighbourhoods, 21, 65, 68
Furedi, Frank, 72, 96

G

Galton, Francis, 53
Gerhardt, Sue, 71
Gillies, Val, 67, 91–2, 96
Greenfield, Susan, 28

H

Harlow, Harry, 44–5
Hart and Risley, 32
Harvard Center on the Developing Child, 21, 34, 68, 100
Hays, Sharon, 10
Head Start and Early Head Start, 65
Heckman, James, 70
HighScope Perry Preschool Project, 73
Hitler, Adolf, 54
Hoskings, George, 69–70

I

I Am Your Child Campaign, 65
implicit to explicit family policy, 64
imprinting, 45
inequality, toxic, 30
instinct, maternal, 13, 48
intimacy, 92

K

Kagan, Jerome, 56, 89, 96, 105, 107
Kant, Immanuel, 50, 51–2
Kids Company, 11, 56, 66
kittens, 44

L

Leach, Penelope, 35, 71
Leadsom, Andrea MP, 70
Lorenz, Konrad, 45
Loughton, Tim MP, 8, 70

M

maternal instinct, 13, 48
mind-minded parenting, 91
modernity, reaction to, 43
monkeys, 44–5
moral entrepreneur, 10, 68
Myth of the First Three Years, 20

N

National Literacy Trust, 79
nature and nurture, 51–3
neuroparenting, definition of, 2
New Deal, 73
Nurse Family Partnership, 73, 86, 97

O

1001 Critical Days, 8, 22, 27, 62, 70, 86, 88
Owen, Robert, 50–1, 52

P

Palmer, Sue, 28
parenting, 3, 6–, 9–10, 15–16
parenting culture studies, 10, 42, 43, 47, 86, 91, 96, 99, 103, 104, 107
parenting deficit, 12–14, 16, 63
parenting support, workforce, expertise, 6, 12, 52, 62–3, 64, 66, 72, 78, 83, 85, 86, 87, 88, 89, 91, 97, 102, 103
Perry, Bruce D., 2, 12, 55–6, 67, 69–70
Perry image, 2, 12
playing, 43, 48–9, 71, 80, 82, 89, 90, 91, 92, 101, 108
pollution, 30
positive parenting, 83–4, 85, 102
postnatal depression, 14, 48, 70, 80, 91, 97–8
primitive, 42
Prince Charles, 10
privacy, 13, 35, 37, 81, 87, 99, 108
Putnam, Robert D., 29, 34, 35, 44, 108

R

rats, 29, 31, 44
ritual magic, 89
rituals, 46, 82, 83, 84, 89–92
Romanian orphanage studies, 36
Rousseau, Jean-Jacques, 49–50, 51, 52

S

scientific motherhood, 54
screens, addition, saturation, mobile phones, 28–9
Sears, 9, 42, 47
sensitive periods, 20, 29, 45
serve and return, 21, 89
Shonkoff, Jack, 21–2, 29, 55, 65, 68
Sigman, Aric, 28, 71
skin-to-skin, 48, 89, 102–3
Starting Points report, 65
still-face paradigm, 90
stimulation, 20, 25, 31, 48–9, 90
Sunderland, Margot, 71
Sure Start, 66, 67, 80, 81, 87, 97
Suskind, Dana, 32
synaptogenesis, 20

T

talking to babies 9, 42, 43, 48–9, 81, 89, 90, 101, 108
technology, screens, mobile phones, 28–9
teenage brain, 86
teenage mothers, 86
therapeutic state, 71–4
Thirty Million Words, 31, 32, 33
Tiger Mom, 30
toxic stress, 2, 21, 34–5, 71, 100
trauma, 12, 15, 55, 84
Tronick, Ed, 90–1

U
underclass, 30, 73

V
vulnerable brain, 22, 26–35, 57

W
War on Poverty, 73
Wave Trust, 69–70
White House conference on the brain, 65
windows of opportunity, 45, 104
wondrous brain, 22–6

Printed by Printforce, the Netherlands